Six Miles from St. Paul

The family and society of Sarah Jane Sibley

By

David M. Grabitske

The Friends of the Sibley Historic Site

Mendota, Minnesota

2008

Six Miles from St. Paul

Copyright © 2008 by David M Grabitske

All rights reserved

Printed in the United States

ISBN: 978-0-692-00069-4

First Printing

Printed by Greenhaven Printing

Layout by Side By Side Marketing

Published by The Friends of the Sibley Historic Site

Mendota, Minnesota

Front Cover:: *A Celebration in Mendota* detail, David P. Geister (2008), private collection. Back Cover: *A Celebration in Mendota*. The painting depicts a scene partly described in a letter from Rachel Steele Johnson in Texas to her sister Sarah Jane Sibley imaging events Johnson probably witnessed many times. The sociable Sibley family often hosted parties and gatherings. In this one, set about 1850, the community of Mendota has gathered. Sarah Jane Sibley sits on the front steps of her family's Mendota home enjoying the antics of her dancing husband "kicking up his heels in the yard" and playing with their children Augusta Ann "Gussie" Sibley and Henry Hastings "Harry" Sibley. Geister's work is done in the Genre style employed by George Caleb Bingham, the most significant American artist throughout Sarah Sibley's life. The population depicted around the Sibley family are many of those that worked with the artist David Geister and David Grabitske, Sarah Jane Sibley's biographer, at Historic Fort Snelling, 1996-1999. The man reading aloud at the top of the steps is Jeff Nordin, who also was the Sibley Historic Site's first site manager. The man peering over Nordin's shoulder is Erik J. Osrud. The military officer is Scott T. Hosier. The man with his back turned to the viewer and wearing a finger woven sash is Mike Sexton as Mr. Perry the Selkirk refugee, a frequent role of his. In front of Sexton and hoisting a beverage is Michael Murray. On the bottom step is Richard A. Williams, the beloved and revered site technician who often could be found managing Historic Fort Snelling as he is shown here. Standing in the distance are John Waldo grinning as he often did, and Matthew W. Hutchinson in his self-described "leprechaun suit." Among the musicians might be recognized Trudi Hoag and Ryan Glomsrud. More fellow interpreters might be seen in the background. At the lower right, David Geister appears sketching the scene of the painting and sitting next to the biographer, David Grabitske.

Illustration credits

Maps on **pages 22-23**: created by David M. Grabitske

Images on **page 39**: photographs by David M. Grabitske; sketch, pencil on paper by Augusta A Sibley, 1856, courtesy Minnesota Historical Society.

Images on **page 40**: Albumen print of Sarah Steele Sibley, 1858, and daguerreotype of Frederick B. Sibley, 1850s, courtesy of Minnesota Historical Society, detail of letter, Sarah Jane Sibley to Ann Pamela Cunningham, July 29, 1859, courtesy of Mount Vernon Ladies Association; photographs of Sarah Jane Sibley's writing desk by David M. Grabitske.

Image on **page 54**: Invitation to Grand Anniversary Ball, Etiquette Items Collection, Minnesota Historical Society.

Images on **page 55**: photographs of china settings and mourning jewelry by David M. Grabitske; lithograph, Residence of General Henry H. Sibley, 417 Woodward, St. Paul courtesy of Minnesota Historical Society.

Images on **page 84**: photographs of the bed, wardrobe, and birdcage by David M. Grabitske; photograph of sewing table courtesy of Minnesota Historical Society.

Images on **pages 106-107**: all courtesy of Minnesota Historical Society.

Family trees on **page 164-165**: courtesy David M. and Hollie A. Grabitske.

Contents

Acknowledgements

My love for history comes from my family. Dad has a bachelor's degree in history. Even though he has spent his life working in other pursuits, he proves to me daily that happiness is a history degree, even if you don't earn a living with it. Mom was a grade school teacher and taught me to love learning. Her good example compelled her to earn a master's degree before she turned 60. So have I. And, my grandmother's brothers, especially Wendal and Ernie Kulenkamp, had a gift for telling true and meaningful stories, which were especially entertaining. I reveled in these at my grandmother's annual Fourth of July picnics in West St. Paul.

The staffers and volunteers at Chester County (PA) Historical Society, Dakota County (MN) Historical Society, Lancaster County (PA) Historical Society, Massachusetts Historical Society, Minnesota Historical Society, Mount Vernon Ladies Association (VA), Ramsey County (MN) Historical Society, Randolph County (IL) Genealogical Society, Washington County (MN) Historical Society, White Bear Lake (MN) Area Historical Society, Winona County (MN) Historical Society, and others materially contributed to the finished product.

Sarah Markoe Hanson and her uncles were especially kind to open their family's papers wherein we discovered her ancestor William Markoe was the one who recruited Sarah for her work with the Mount Vernon Ladies Association. Among Sarah's family, Sandy Elmstrom and Bruce Kohn were most gracious and hospitable.

The extensive network of Minnesota historians, both independent and at the Minnesota Historical Society, constantly encouraged me to keep at it (and to finish). There are really too many to mention, but of particular note: Annette Atkins, Robert Averbeck, Marjorie Bingham, John Lansing Callaghan, Roberta Everling, Timothy C. Glines, Anne Kaplan, Corinne Marz, Patrick McCormack, Deborah L. Miller, Robert and Marveen Minish, Stephen E. Osman, Ann Regan, Susan Roth, Bruce White, Alan Woolworth, George Woytanowitz. The namesake Sarah Steele Sibley Chapter of the DAR (and the other Minnesota chapters) further supported and encouraged this work by inviting me to present Sarah's story. And, my sincere thanks to the Friends of the Sibley Historic Site who enthusiastically embraced publishing the book.

Special thanks to the two who designed the book: Dan Seidler of Side by Side Marketing for his layout of the book, and David P. Geister for his long friendship and original painting on the cover.

Finally, if it were not for site manager Lisa A. Krahn and my fellow guides at the Sibley House Historic Site, this project would never have been conceived as it has been. If any of this story is useful or interesting, I sincerely hope the reader will take the time to seek out Sarah, especially at her Mendota home, and really talk with the guides about this fascinating woman.

Lastly, though she came to this project at the end, the contributions of my wife Hollie are most deeply appreciated.

Chapter 1: My Youngest Sister Accompanying Us

Sarah Jane Sibley loved her family and friends. Socializing with others engaged her curiosity, humor, skills, taste, and style. In short, Sarah thrived on community, particularly on the close friendships with her sisters.

Yet Sarah Sibley lived in Mendota for most of her life in Minnesota. Mendota was beyond the head of navigation on the Mississippi River. When Minnesota was opened to settlement by whites, many people stopped at St. Paul, which was six miles downstream and across the river from Mendota. Sarah felt isolated from her broader society of family and friends.

Still, early settlers knew her and admired her. Despite how well Sarah knew her peers, how well known she was by the society in which she moved, and the level of prominence to which she rose, Sarah is perhaps only remembered as the wife of Henry Hastings Sibley. Over time, Minnesotans have lost their knowledge of Sarah Jane Sibley.

But one look at a map of Minnesota is enough to suggest the name Sibley is connected to the state's development and history. Sibley County in the south central agricultural region is nestled just above the great bend of the Minnesota River, which forms the county's irregular eastern boundary. The county is surrounded by others bearing the names of Nicollet, Brown, Renville, and McLeod – all named for men associated with the Sibley name.

Whether planned that way or not, Henry Hastings Sibley and his wife Sarah Jane were at the center of this society of pioneers just as the county that shares the family name remains in the center of those named for their colleagues, friends, employees, and social circle. This circle of counties is woven together by the Minnesota River, which the Dakota named for its turbulent look, cloudy waters. The ironic symbolism of this south central area embodies the story of Minnesota at its creation.

As residents of Mendota (another anglicized Dakota term meaning "confluence"), Henry and Sarah Sibley continue to color the local community. Just a mile from their first home together, where they began their family, Henry Sibley High School in Mendota Heights bears passive witness to their commitment to education, learning, and culture. Across the Mississippi River Valley Gorge, below St. Paul's Highland Park area, is Sibley Plaza, a commercial marketplace offering a multitude of shops suggesting the Sibleys' involvement with and development of the new state's economy. In St. Paul, just six miles downstream from their first home, a major street leading from the river into the heart of Lowertown, where they eventually settled, bears their name. Whether living in or visiting Minnesota, one cannot escape a confluence with the name Sibley.

Henry Hastings Sibley was born in Detroit, Michigan Territory, just ahead of the War of 1812, to a father who labored for the creation of the State of Michigan as strenuously as his son did a generation later for the State of Minnesota. Rhoda Gilman's 2004 biography of Henry Sibley demonstrates from his papers and other manuscripts a very complex man with a heart divided. Sibley negotiated between the necessities of business and his American Indian clients. He had strong family ties and yet loved his independence. Just as he saw the inexorable march of American development and eventual displacement of his American Indian relatives, Sibley's loyalty to his Dakota relatives were constrained by American Victorian sensibilities. While Sibley was loyal to his white in-laws, still he felt duty-bound to national political figures in the face of a disintegrating nation. Above all Sibley seems a man of and ahead of his times who had an increasingly progressive outlook. Sibley searched for a way that made sense to him to negotiate the cloudy waters of his circumstances.

Gilman's compassionate view of Henry Sibley stands in marked difference to other portraits of the man. Sibley's own veiled picture of himself shows a modest participant, with only hints of what he really thought about the events of his life, and only partly discloses the length and breadth of his involvement. Nathaniel West's biography written toward the end of Sibley's life is more florid prose than candid analysis, and paints Sibley with a near baronial existence deeply respected for his long experience, venerated for his mighty deeds on behalf of a grateful populace, and sought out for an opinion that weighed heavily. The Minnesota Daughters of the American Revolution (DAR) elevated West's lofty status of Sibley to that of George Washington, a self-made man of the west who magnanimously used his talents and position for the good of society. In marketing the Sibley House as a must-see historic site, the DAR christened it the "Mount Vernon of Minnesota." Though wrapped in patriotism and glory by succeeding generations, as Gilman shows, Sibley was like any of us: doubtful and sure, loving and heartless, confused and clear, all depending on the circumstances.

Six Miles from St. Paul

The Minnesota of Sibley's early adulthood beckoned him with outdoor pleasures of bucolic lakes teeming with fish and birds, sinewy streams providing access to oceans of wide, gently rolling prairies as lushly beautiful as the bodies of water, and boundless adventure chasing game with dogs, horses, and firearms. The majesty of broad expanses of sky held clear, blue days with wisps of clouds that could turn on rising humidity into pea-green calamity in summer or sudden white fury in wintry blizzards. The rapid evolution of seasons and weather conditions still draws Minnesotans to their natural environment. Once Sarah Jane Steele married Henry Sibley, what beckoned him held her. Sarah would enjoy the environment through horticulture, animal husbandry, accompanying her husband on hunts near their home, and during pleasure rides in their carriage and on horseback.

Although Henry Sibley's papers survive, they only survive in part as the donor restriction on them required the return of personal papers. Those returned papers were destroyed by his surviving children because of a Victorian respect for marital privacy that they felt should be held sacred for all time. As the majority of his wife Sarah's identity was wrapped in the family, marriage, children and home, her story perished at the hands of her own children. Sarah's life prior to marriage was as a daughter of a prominent Pennsylvania politician and industrialist, James Steele. His papers likewise are not available – the last known location being in the possession of Sarah's brother James Steele in Coulterville, Illinois, in 1881. Therefore, at first glance Sarah Sibley's life appears fragmentary, hinting at the possibility of suggestion, and as a shadowy wallflower hovering at the edge of her husband's public life. Sarah was far from being a wallflower in her husband's life. Rather, she was a woman of accomplishment in her own right.

If life involves a negotiation between the circumstances under which we live, and between the choices we make to change circumstances, then no less is true for Sarah Jane Steele in the early and mid-nineteenth century. Tall and slender, Sarah learned her sense of place from her parents and relatives, from whom she studied skills necessary for life. What Sarah learned as a child shaped her future and prepared her for relationships, to manage a household, and to be a leader. Her choices likewise shaped the character of her adopted state, delicately broadening women's public roles, and supported a nascent historic preservation movement. Reasonable and value-based choices for Sarah Sibley enabled her to negotiate the questions presented to her. She chose to go west, marry a rising star with whom she could achieve goals, build a household comprising a large family and staff, superintend a complex fundraising campaign against long odds, and position her family for their combined good and success.

When Sarah was born on February 8, 1823, the United States of America faced the waning of the Early Republic on the doorstep of the Jacksonian Era, during which Sarah lived most of her life. The Early Republic glowed with the optimism that finally a government existed in which men could govern themselves. Old institutions from an old world would not hinder a natural drive for improvement in all fields of endeavor. What the new methods would be continued to change with each experiment and mostly resembled what had been before despite incessant tinkering. If in seeming approbation of the unfettered feelings of the era, when Sarah was three years old, Thomas Jefferson and John Adams, leaders in the Revolution and two subsequent Presidents, died on the glorious national holiday of July 4 – God seemingly announced his favor of the new country he established in the Revolution and preserved in the War of 1812. No doubt Sarah's parents and their generation reflected on the momentous events of their lives over meals and family times imbuing Sarah and her siblings with the belief of the American Dream in the face of terrifying contemporary uncertainties, tumultuous frontier conditions, and implacable opposition on the world stage.

Sarah's grandparents William Steele and Rachel Carr relocated to Pennsylvania from Virginia and had six children. All four of their sons helped the American Revolution succeed against Great Britain. The oldest son, Archibald, rose to the rank of colonel, and long held the position of military storekeeper in Philadelphia until discharged in 1821. His legendary exploits in Benedict Arnold's expedition that failed to add Canada to the United States still serve as an example of sacrifice and endurance. Overloaded transports began to sink during the December crossing of the St. Lawrence, such that Archibald threw himself in the frigid water and clung to the gunwales while his comrades held onto his hands until the command reached shore. The resulting near-hypothermia and privations of subsequent captivity debilitated his health for the remainder of his life. He died about three months prior to Sarah's birth, at 80 years of age.

Second son William Steele participated in the Revolution as a newlywed, having married Elizabeth Bailey on September 14, 1775. Elizabeth's parents Robert Bailey and Margaret McDill were among the prominent founders of Lancaster whose children intermarried with the Steeles, including Archibald and William's sister Rachel who married Elizabeth's brother, Jacob Bailey. In addition to building up Lancaster, the Baileys were active in the Middle Octoraro Presbyterian Church just as the Steeles were.

Third son John Steele became a member of the exclusive Society of the Cincinnati, open only to officers of the Revolution and their male descendants. John suffered grievous and presumably mortal wounds at Brandywine in 1777, not far from the family home to which he was taken to die. Recovering, he went on to command Martha Washington's bodyguard, serve as a Brigadier General, and stand by George Washington's side at the surrender of British forces under Lord General Cornwallis at Yorktown in 1781.

After the war he married Abigail Bailey, a sister of Elizabeth and Jacob. John and Abigail were neighbors and partners with Sarah's parents along the Octoraro Creek. They built a stone house with a slate roof in which they raised their seven children – Sarah Jane's cousins. James' brother, John Steele, owned and operated the papermill with a mill race parallel to and fed by the Octoraro. Originally destined to be a minister, John's love of learning prompted him and Abigail to print the first American edition of *Dillworth's Spelling Book*. John died shortly after Sarah's fourth birthday, and his wife Abigail died just 19 days later.

William and Rachel's youngest child was James Steele. Although born in 1763, James still managed to participate in the Revolution, though not in the audacious capacity as did his brothers. As an 18-year-old freshly commissioned lieutenant, he was with his company in Baltimore en route to Yorktown when they received word of the surrender. All things considered, the company decided to return home without ever seeing their enemy. James Steele again answered his country's call during the second war with Great Britain in 1812, when he served his state as Inspector General of Pennsylvania Troops. James Steele's public service also encompassed elective office in the Pennsylvania legislature and public works projects in roads and an 1841 bridge over the Octoraro Creek of the settlement of Steelesville.

The heroic self-sacrifice of her uncles and the unwavering public service tradition of Sarah's family imprinted itself on the next generation. Of Sarah and her siblings, one became a doctor who served terms as city physician, three married politicians (governor, city president, and gubernatorial candidate), and one sacrificed her dreams and happiness to nurse aging parents.

John and James Steele harnessed the swift-flowing Octoraro Creek for three mills near Thompson's Ford northwest of Philadelphia following the War of 1812 – one that made paper and two that produced cotton fabric. The small community of laborers that sprang up around the mills was named in their honor, Steelesville. Sarah's father James Steele wed Mary H. Humes in 1800. Close-knit family relations shaped by legendary public service, familiarity with industrial waterpower for an emerging, self-confident nation, and respect for education were all parts of Sarah's experience growing up.

James Steele was said to be "universally beloved," with a talent for connecting to people that propelled him into the Pennsylvania legislature. "Universally beloved" was the term people of Sarah's generation applied to socially adroit citizens whose amiable motives had the public good at heart. As he was a noted equestrian, neighbors could easily distinguish him at a distance on his famous big gray horse; and the compliment "to ride like Steele" was taken as a superlative. Sarah's first historian Julia Johnson wrote that "Humor was one of the prime luxuries ... in that other genial home in Lancaster." In an age of speeches, the fodder of the Steele family's deeds colored by a sense of the dramatic and a tasteful touch of humor enthralled listeners. Good standing in the community and a popular, fun-loving, gregarious natured love of talking marked the family of Sarah's youth.

James and Mary Steele raised nine children, and Sarah was the last. While her oldest sibling Elizabeth died as an infant, William, James, John, Mary, Franklin, Rachel, and Abbian were all part of Sarah's childhood. Apparently "Bill" and "Frank" followed closely in their father's work at the family's two cotton mills. That closeness prompted an unquestioned desire for the comfort of other family members. John attended medical school in Lancaster, and Mary, or "Moll" as she was called, became a nurse for her elderly father and later her mother. Having a large and close family was certainly part of Sarah's circumstances, and one that she valued. (1)

The exact nature of Sarah's training is unknown, but fragmentary evidence clearly indicates at least some of her training. The ideal well-trained female of the day was one who was content with her lot in life, who cheerfully preserved the happiness of her family, and who had unlimited hospitality and great tact. Sarah certainly demonstrated all of these. For much of her married life she was content and hospitable in her Mendota home, even though she preferred to move to St. Paul. She often interceded in disputes and created happy resolutions. Sarah strived to be the ideal of her day.

To move in the circles she inhabited, Sarah learned some very necessary skills and other attainments. The few surviving letters show a legible and steady hand, and that she had the difficult ability to cross-write. In an age on the verge of typewriters and long before keyboards and word processing, penmanship marked a person as a professional with skills as important as the ability to craft the spoken word for audiences. Clarity in communication commanded and informed public opinion. Sarah's choice of words and deft turns of phrases demonstrate a widely read intellectual who chooses what she writes with care and purpose. Yet she also used contractions such as "dont" without the apostrophe at a time when such contractions were new. It seems she wrote as she might have spoken, in a rather educated but informal manner.

Sarah had a sense of art. In one surviving drawing when she was about twelve, Sarah drew a self-portrait in a popular style of the day. She had a good eye for photography, as a married woman telling her husband, "I took [daughter] Guss with me [to St. Paul] and had her likeness taken – a pretty good one I think." She combined her artistic eye and vocabulary to write at least three surviving poems. And her acute sense of design enabled her to create her own stylish wardrobe and to wear it with a "personal dignity that commanded respect from all classes." That sense of fashion assisted her as she redecorated her Mendota home when her husband retired from the fur trade and politics in 1853. Likewise, her delicate and graceful jewelry also demonstrates her refined tastes in the way she would accent her presentation. (2)

One talent Sarah did not have was singing. Sarah later was amazed her when daughter Augusta found this talent, causing Sarah to remark to her sister Rachel, "It does not seem in the family to be musical, well we cant tell what your voice or mine would have been if they had been brought out." No doubt Sarah did sing in church, which she attended frequently. Voice was as important as the ability to speak or write or perform well for a public audience in the nineteenth century. In fact, any endeavor performed in the face of the public was expected to be accomplished appropriately or not at all, and Sarah was not inclined to begin so late in life. Therefore Sarah and Rachel would never know what the quality of their voices could have been. Yet sister Abbian seems to have played a melodeon. And Sarah hints in her letters of her knowledge of dance. So, despite Sarah's modesty, the family had some musical skills. (3)

Sarah loved animals, and probably learned that from her father. Like her father, she became an accomplished equestrian enjoying her rides through the countryside. And, as she loved horses, she also loved raising animals. Her circa 1835 self-portrait shows her with a pet dog suggesting the family of her youth had dogs at least as cherished pets if not also working animals on their farm. Although she loved dogs, later on as a wife managing a household, she could not allow dogs in her house if she were to have any chance of keeping the house clean. So, upon her marriage, her husband's twelve hunting dogs were moved from the house to a kennel. Sibley's prized hunting dog, Lion, subsequently escaped the kennel and lived out his life across the river at Fort Snelling.

As Minnesota approached statehood, Sarah raised chickens to have a steady supply of eggs for sale and occasional dinner meat. She even sold some of her chickens to her friends William and Mary LeDuc, promising them to "send written directions for their treatment by the first opportunity." Growing up in the largely rural town of Steelesville gave her the opportunity to learn about animal husbandry, gardening, and agriculture. Living as a married woman in the similarly rural town of Mendota in Minnesota gave her the opportunity to practice those skills. (4)

Like many middle class young women of her day, Sarah also attended a finishing school. There is no record of which finishing school, but there were many in Philadelphia and Baltimore that she may have attended. Typical finishing school curricula included training in the many talents and skills Sarah demonstrated throughout her married life such as expertise in sewing, cultured manners, and adroit penmanship.

Sarah's formal education concluded in the spring of 1842 when her brother Frank returned from "the St. Peter's" — as the area around Mendota and Fort Snelling was known — on business. Frank's business apparently also included finding a spouse. He traveled with a friend of his, Henry Hastings Sibley, who was headed for Washington City in the District of Columbia to lobby for the passage of the 1841 treaty with the Dakota. The two men may well have stopped in Lancaster and Steelesville, Pennsylvania, as these towns are on the way from the west to the nation's capital via Philadelphia. Along the way the two men made a friendly wager about who might marry first.

From Philadelphia, Steele coyly wrote Sibley with well-honed Steele humor on April 6, "Now my Dear Sir I have something to communicate that will make you open your eyes. What do you think it is? Why it is nothing more or less than that your friend Steele take with him to the west a partner for life." Steele went on to tease Sibley "don't be surprised when I inform you that it is Miss B." Annie Barney came from a distinguished Baltimore family that was also well known in the Lancaster-Philadelphia area. Her grandfather was Supreme Court Associate Justice Samuel Chase, a signer of the Declaration of Independence, who remains the only justice on that court impeached. Annie's sister Frances Chase Barney had married the son of one of Frank and Sarah's cousins, William Porter Steele, so it is fairly likely the family assisted Frank in making the arrangement possible, or that Frank knew Annie well before he left for the west. All the same, Frank's business acumen for contractual details prompted him to playfully close his letter to Sibley, "Allow me to remind you that you are under obligations [of our wager] to have Mrs. Sibley at St. Peters upon the arrival of Mrs. Steele." Frank well knew Sibley would not have a wife there on his return. However, perhaps Frank was aware he was bringing the future Mrs. Sibley as he promised to "immediately leave for the west my youngest Sister accompanying us." (5)

Henry Sibley boarded the morning train from Washington to Baltimore on Thursday, April 14, 1842, for the wedding later in the day. He graciously served his friend Frank as Best Man in the wedding, and if he had not before, certainly met Frank's youngest sister, Sarah Jane. The details of the wedding are scant, but if it was similar to others of the day it would have occurred in the parlor of a relative's house, most likely Annie's parents' home, with only a few close family members in attendance. One might easily imagine Steele's tall, handsome groomsman beguiling the equally refined and charming Sarah during the social moments that followed a brief ceremony. The bond between Sarah and Henry grew from that April day. (6)

Frank purposefully mentioned Sarah would accompany him and Annie, which must have been news Henry hoped to hear. The passage certainly suggests that Henry knew Sarah before April of 1842, that Sarah had not planned on going to Fort Snelling, and that she had changed her mind about where she would live in the near term. Frank's announcement suggests that Sarah and Henry may have been attracted to each other.

Business delayed Frank from returning to Fort Snelling as soon as he planned, and Henry Sibley arrived at the St. Peter's first. As historian and DAR regent Katherine Vaughan described, Henry passed time on a buffalo hunt on which he was injured to the extent he was unable to move about easily. However, the officers teasingly observed that he made some kind of a miraculous recovery to pay a visit to Sarah soon after her arrival at Fort Snelling along with her brother and sister-in-law. Sibley's business partner Hercules Dousman further teased him as the courtship that winter progressed: "the officers have had a report for some time that you were Steeling."(7)

All the pieces were in place for Sarah's married life. She had been reared in a small village essentially run by her father and relatives. She would soon live in a small village essentially run by her husband. Her education prepared her to lead society in the Fort Snelling-Mendota area, and that education also whetted her appetite for society and refinement of urban areas such as St. Paul. However, being early on the scene, she would gain popularity, as her father had with a quick wit, boundless capacity for amusement, and engaging stories. Those former associations in Pennsylvania would shortly assure her and her family of continued access to the highest levels of the nascent Minnesota society. That training prepared her to manage a complex household of family, guests, and employees all constituting her primary society. The broader society would demand that Sarah use her knowledge and talents to lead them through an early effort at historic preservation and fundraising. That training bolstered her courage to manage and lead, which increased her social capital when she convinced other relatives to join her in Minnesota.

The choices she made to accompany her brother to the west, to take a chance on Henry Sibley far from the bulk of her relatives, and to remain in the west reveal a certain level of confidence in her own abilities not seconded by remaining fragmentary sources.

Key to letters on map:

S = Sibley Houses
P = Potts House
H = Helen Hastings Sibley (living as Wm. R. Brown)
ER = Edmund Rice
FH = Fuller House (where Gov. Sibley boarded)
JP = John Prince
C = St. Paul Episcopal Church
J = Dr. John Steele

Chapter 2: Not After All So Very Unpleasant

Sarah's introduction to the community of Fort Snelling in the fall of 1842 was auspicious and certainly prescient of further excitement to come from the Steele girls. On their arrival, Henry Sibley was summoned in his capacity as Justice of the Peace for Clayton County, Iowa Territory, to inspect an alleged peephole created by Rev. Benjamin Kavanaugh between his cabin and the newlywed Steeles. Sibley filed an affidavit, and Kavanaugh shortly resigned his call to the Methodist Red Rock Mission in modern Newport. (8)

Sarah Jane Sibley probably weathered the Kavanaugh scandal, as Sarah's first historian Julia M. Johnson wrote, with "ready jest and capacity for amusement." She balanced concern for others' well-being - genuine interest in their stories – with her deep humility, contentment and happiness. Diligent in reading her Bible, Sarah knew the exhortations of Proverbs 31:10-31 praising the admirable qualities to be found in a wife and likely felt responsible for meeting those expectations. Johnson, in writing of Sarah's positive attitude, acknowledged that Sarah tried to meet the feminine ideal of a happy disposition reflective of Proverbs 31:25, "Strength and honor are her clothing, and she shall rejoice in time to come." Or as historian Elizabeth Donaghy Garrett quipped, "One of the first trials to a little girl's temper was the lesson that she wasn't supposed to have much of a temper at all." Sarah's disposition was critical to the success of all of the relationships she inspired. (9)

Although the close-knit community around the St. Peter's seemed similar to the one she grew up in around the Octoraro Creek, Mendota was vastly different from southeastern Pennsylvania. The unfettered openness of the prairie with very few trees was not like the tree-lined lanes leading to culture in urban settings, which were an easy journey from her parents' house. Rivers and streams substituted as roads, and great distances prohibited spur-of-the-moment visits to the outside world.

On winter's doorstep when she arrived, her new world must have seemed at once curious and bleak. The clockwork life within the military post was alien to most Americans, and usually treated as a spectacle as it was rarely witnessed by the public. The government commonly stationed its professional soldiers either in coastal installations or on the national frontiers. Thus, seeing the military was unusual for most Americans. As opposed to the rough caliber of men in the ranks, refined officers, some, accompanied by their wives, affected the same cultured manners Sarah practiced.

Among the officers, she founded new relationships that helped her learn what each knew of Mr. Sibley. He had long formed a strong society of friends among the officers with whom he hunted, dined, attended parties, bred and raced horses, and pursued many other interests. Sibley also maintained business licenses with the Indian Agent, which was a requirement of his profession that brought him often to Fort Snelling.

For Sarah to end the year in a strange environment that was preparing for winter must have reminded her of the end of her girlhood and suggested the following spring could witness the beginning of her womanhood. So Sarah Jane Steele moved into the small but fashionable cottage with her brother and his wife just south of the walls of the fort where Frank owned the exclusive right to operate the sutler store. Sutler stores provided soldiers who had permission to spend their pay on items not supplied by the government. Despite the granted monopoly such stores were not guaranteed successes for the entrepreneurs who owned them. Though she perhaps granted Sibley a monopoly on her heart, that did not guarantee him success.

Throughout the winter, Sarah received Sibley on visits, and presumably paid them in turn in company with her brother Frank to Sibley's fur post across the river from Fort Snelling as they forged their relationship. Sarah could readily compare the industrial complex of her father's mills with her suitor's fur post. Her father's mills contained gritty workmen, piles of waste, and the hum of comings and goings of draymen. Despite being experienced with such working areas, at the fur post Sarah would have been understandably shocked by the omnipresent smell of rotting flesh in the near half-million drying pelts of dead animals awaiting shipment downstream for processing into things she and her family would buy in the stores of Philadelphia. The noise of oxcarts with greaseless wheels turning on wooden axels could be heard for miles. The fur post's noise and smell must have been astonishing.

Comings and goings here were perhaps more significant than at her father's mills, for in remote Mendota travelers of any kind also brought news from afield. Her keen interest in the world around her, skills at hospitality, and conversational abilities would aid Sarah in participating fully with visitors.

Her husband's laborers must have presented an exotic vision of colorful dress, customs, religion, and habits. She likely had learned French in school, but how much of the country patois she understood is unknown. The rhythmic songs of the trade repeated lines that all the men could echo with gusto, much like the songs of sailors and laborers Sarah probably witnessed visiting Philadelphia while growing up. The manner of dress with its color soon revealed to Sarah the order of these men, which was probably not entirely dissimilar to the adornment that distinguished Americans in the east.

But the greatest difference existed in their religion. While Catholicism was not unknown in the United States, it certainly was not as prevalent as it was on the St. Peter's. Learning the various feast days may have required some patience. Becoming accustomed to the misrule tradition invoked for major celebrations may have been harder still. Misrule is the right of revelers to impose on a host for some treat or favor, much as is still practiced on Halloween. Certainly such a practice must have tried Sarah's patience.

Elizabeth Pelagie Faribault, who went by her middle name and Sibley's next door neighbor's wife, was a 59 year-old mother of eight children in 1842 when Sarah arrived. Sibley's close relationship with the Faribault family, particularly son Alexander Faribault, no doubt introduced Sarah to this noble family. The scion of the family was 67-year-old Jean-Baptiste, whose father had come to Quebec shortly before the French and Indian War. Born in 1775, Jean-Baptiste Faribault entered into the fur trade in 1798, and was present during U.S. Army Lieutenant Zebulon Pike's 1805 negotiations with the Dakota on the big island in the Mississippi River for land to build a fort. Pelagie married Jean-Baptiste Faribault the same year as Pike's visit. Her relatives included both Mdewakanton Dakota and French. She married "in the fashion of the country"; that is, without the blessing of a Christian church. But she had her marriage blessed by a Catholic priest from St. Louis who visited Prairie du Chien where they resided in 1817.

Pelagie's son Alexander Faribault married Mary Elizabeth Graham, who like her mother-in-law went by her middle name. A year older than her husband, Elizabeth Faribault was a 37 year-old mother of seven children, the oldest of whom was two years younger than Sarah herself. Like her mother-in-law, Elizabeth was the daughter of a Dakota woman and a European, Captain Duncan Graham from Great Britain.

Elizabeth Faribault's sister-in-law Lucy-Anne Faribault married Henry Sibley's predecessor, fur company trader Alexis Bailly in 1826. Lucy was a 33 year-old mother, also of seven children. Bailly, like his father-in-law Jean-Baptiste, was descended from Frenchmen, but unlike his father-in-law, Bailly had the good fortune to have been born in the United States. Following the War of 1812, American law prohibited foreigners from participating in the fur trade on U.S. soil. Thus Jean-Baptiste Faribault became a naturalized citizen in 1816. (10)

How Sarah socialized with Pelagie and Elizabeth Faribault and Lucy Bailly is not known. It is hard to imagine in a small community that Sarah did not seek their companionship. Sarah must have looked to these women for their wisdom and counsel to integrate with existing society and to learn how to behave among the Dakota, and for insight into what lay ahead in married life.

Perhaps it was these women with family connections to the Dakota who brought the matter of Henry Sibley's own Dakota daughter to Sarah's attention. Or it could have been the officers who also knew Sibley well. When Sarah learned of Helen Hastings Sibley's existence, or what her immediate reaction to the news might have been, are unknown. Sarah most likely did not learn of Helen until she arrived at Fort Snelling in the fall of 1842.

Helen had been born to Red Blanket Woman, likely on August 28, 1841. Red Blanket Woman was a member of Black Dog's clan, and, as a Mdewakanton, spent much of the year in the vicinity of Sibley's Mendota trading post. She probably met Sibley during a hunt he spent with the Dakota. Historians Bruce Kohn and Alan Woolworth, among others, pieced together much of Helen's story from fragmentary evidence including the notes of Return Ira Holcombe, who originally organized the Sibley Papers. Muzzawakanwin (euphemistically: trader's daughter or hunter's daughter), as Helen was known to her Dakota relatives, grew up in the family of William and Martha Brown, who served the Methodist mission at Red Rock (modern Newport, Minnesota). Though one reference suggests Sarah harbored hard feelings about her stepdaughter, those feelings did not prohibit Helen from knowing her father, or perhaps meeting her half-siblings.

Sarah Jane may also have learned that Henry Sibley had many "sweets," as Hercules Dousman alluded to in one letter to Henry, and further hinted of his "long experience in the Indian Trade." Dr. Thomas S. Williamson, a missionary to the Dakota and friend of Sibley's, wrote to Sibley that he hoped "that you are again living in communion with the Father of all our mercies who of his infinite goodness always kindly welcomes the returning wanderer." Williamson knew of Sibley's "ample experience" in "worldly amusements." Some scholars allege that Sibley had more than one Dakota child. While it is difficult to interpret Dousman and Williamson's remarks precisely, it seems likely that Sibley had multiple sexual partners, and possibly more than one child, prior to Sarah arriving in Mendota. (11)

Whatever she learned over the winter of 1842-1843 did not dissuade Sarah from marrying Henry Sibley. The situation and context of the transparent society around the St. Peter's must have given her at least a brief pause and a lot to digest and consider. Any misgivings she held or deception she perceived must have been balanced by possibilities and promise for good years ahead.

Sarah Jane Steele wed Henry Hastings Sibley on May 2, 1843, in the schoolhouse (which doubled as a chapel) at Fort Snelling. Like her brother Frank's wedding, the details of the Sibley wedding only note the date and place, and that Rev. Ezekiel Gilbert Gear officiated. Gear was a Presbyterian minister who in 1838 came to serve the congregation at Fort Snelling organized three years before. Sibley had made a public profession of his

Christian faith at a Presbyterian meeting while on Mackinac Island in 1830. Organizing St. Peter's Church five years later at Fort Snelling with army officers Gustavus Loomis and Ned Ogden, Sibley served as a ruling elder from then until he formally withdrew from the congregation in 1849. He built a church in Mendota in 1845, which probably was the main reason he and Sarah did not attend services across the river. St. Peter's Church congregation moved a couple times prior to taking root in Minneapolis as First Presbyterian, arguably the oldest organized Christian congregation in Minnesota. (12)

The house into which Sarah moved when she married Henry was not built as a residence, but as a commercial building. Construction probably began, or at least was planned, in 1836, certainly much of it was paid for in 1838 and probably concluded in 1839. Henry had lived here as a bachelor, and converting a place of business to a home would take every domestic skill Sarah possessed.

John Muller, the original builder from the Red River Selkirk colony, carefully crafted the stout masonry walls, probably with the work actually performed soldiers from Fort Snelling. The base of the walls measure approximately four feet thick and taper from basement to the roof on the inside while maintaining plumb on the exterior. At each floor the walls have a shelf on which the beams supporting the floors rest. The basement held the kitchen with its hearth and two larder (or pantry) chambers. Each larder's floor is slightly lower than the basement floor and accessed by a small door to the kitchen. Under the floors Muller ingeniously incorporated drains to carry off melting ice, and to assist the spring thaw in the bluffs above the house that might raise the water table under the house.

The original part of the house is nearly a perfect square. On the first floor, a large room on the northeast hosted the business of the fur trade. Ledgers documenting transactions sat in a large safe, and a clerk's desk with pigeon holes would have been the focal point – all amid manufactured wares, bulk foods, and sundry items. Behind this room were two smaller store rooms. One store room on the southeast corner had a door facing south. The main door to the building was in the opposite corner, which entered into a foyer outside both the commercial room and the southwest store room.

For living quarters, Sibley and his guests accessed the second floor by an exterior stair on the southwest side of the building. On ascending the stair, a door opened on another foyer that had doors leading to the attic, to Sibley's apartment over the commercial room, and to a room that ran the length of the south side of the house. The ideal in architecture at that time demanded balance, and while the floorplan usually had rooms balance each other on each floor, the Sibley house's rooms balance each other from the first floor to the second.

Certainly the Sibley house was built for commerce. Reusing a building can be a challenge, but the Sibleys decided to make the best of it and reuse the stone commercial building as a family residence. They probably made plans to adaptively reuse the house their first summer together, and Henry used much of the first year to gather resources needed to begin the construction project.

With plans progressing for an addition to both his family and his home, Henry took Sarah (then 5 months pregnant) and their servant girl on a trip to Detroit in the winter of 1843-44 to introduce her to his family. Her new Detroit relations fondly welcomed her into a family that already boasted two Sarah Sibleys. Her mother-in-law Sarah Whipple Sproat was a 62-year-old granddaughter of Commodore Abraham Whipple, a hero of the American Revolution. She married Solomon Sibley, eleven years her senior, in Marietta, Ohio, in late 1802. The senior Mrs. Sibley bore eight children.

Her firstborn son Ebenezer Sproat Sibley entered West Point the same year Sarah Jane was born, graduating first in his class in 1827. When Sproat, as his family called him, gained his new sister-in-law, he was a 37-year-old bachelor and brevet captain of artillery stationed in Savannah, Georgia. As with all the Sibley brothers, Sproat was tall and powerfully built. One biographer noted his "iron constitution" that served him well throughout his 41-year career in the military. At the time of Henry and Sarah's marriage, he had completed one tour of duty in the Seminole War in Florida and would shortly see service in Texas and the subsequent War with Mexico. (13)

Two more brothers, Alexander Hamilton Sibley and Frederick B. Sibley, were, like Sproat, bachelors. While Alexander would marry Marie Miller later in the 1860s, Fred remained single his whole life. Henry's beloved youngest brother Fred, affable, sensitive and the baby of the family, was exactly 16 months younger than Sarah Jane, which probably encouraged his liberal teasing of her. (14)

Henry's oldest sister, 36 year-old Catherine Whipple Sibley, was the second child in the family, and the first to get married. The socially popular Kate had married Charles Trowbridge in 1826, and undoubtedly delighted in welcoming her new sister-in-law. Both Kate and Sarah Jane proved a flair for managing balls and parties and probably were close friends. Charlie Trowbridge met Kate when she was a student of his sister Eliza. Another sister, Mary Sibley, would marry Charles Adams, the other half of the affectionately referred to "two Charlies."

Henry's youngest sister was another Sarah Sibley. Sarah Augustine Sibley was just older than Sarah Jane Sibley and something of an artist who loved to sing. Her brother Henry sent her ermine that she had made into a fashionable muff and shawl for winter wear.

On their return to Mendota, Henry apologized in a letter to his brother Fred, "The girl we brought along did nothing but grumble all the time." Domestic help would prove to be a chronic problem during their married life. Henry and Sarah seemingly had little success in reforming their servant's attitude, as "she has not yet got straight." Since Sarah was five months pregnant during the trip to meet her in-laws, it was important to have good help, so she hired "another woman also."

The trip home also tried Sarah's patience. Henry noted to Fred in the same letter, that at "Prairie du Chien, the weather [was] extremely Stormy & boistrous." While there, they "resided with Mr. & Mrs. [Daniel] Fenton who treated us with much attention & kindness." Sibley acknowledged how difficult Sarah found sleeping "in the same room with half a dozen men," and harder still to "make her toilette in their presence." Henry undoubtedly wishfully supposed that "she soon became accustomed to it," reporting that Sarah "speaks of her travels as not after all so very unpleasant." Trained and cultured as she was, Sarah definitely maintained a preference for certain standards but probably made the best of the situation in February 1844 as there was little she could do to change the circumstances. (15)

The one set of circumstances she could change comprised the living arrangements in the former commercial building they intended to reuse as a house. In 1844 John Muller returned to ply his craft on an addition to the south or rear side, meant to rehabilitate the building for use as a proper house.

By building onto the rear, the exit from the basement now led directly into the house. Common houses of the day did not typically have a direct link to the kitchen inside the house. Meals prepared in the basement were either consumed there or taken outside first before presentation in a dining room in order to keep as much of the mess of cooking from getting into difficult-to-clean upholstery, drapes, and other textiles. Before his marriage, Henry Sibley and his guests likely took their meals in the basement, an arrangement that would not do in a house of his family's station.

The rooms of the addition provided functionality to the home missing in the original commercial building. Sarah probably found the modern warming kitchen useful for light tasks such as ironing, raising dough for bread, making tea, or keeping subsequent meal courses ready adjacent to the dining room. Servants and the Sibley children took their meals in the warming kitchen. The coals from its stove could be used in bed warming pans. The other room in the addition hosted the dining room, the scene of many dinners with both important and ordinary visitors. The door from the southeast storeroom to the outside now became the portal between the dining room and great hall.

The Sibleys reused the original rooms on the first floor. The two storerooms on the south side were merged into one great hall. The east window became a new door to the outside. It, and the window on the west, were the only sources of light. Eliminating the other two openings (now doors to the addition) made the great hall a significantly darker space. Nevertheless, this long room with wicker chairs along its sides could host large social gatherings. The commercial room converted nicely to a proper parlor, the venue for at least two weddings and likely many Sunday family gatherings. Both foyers were partly sacrificed to allow an interior stair to the second floor.

Sibley's second floor apartment became the master bedroom. The long south room continued as before, no doubt with portable partitions to give the space maximum flexibility. Added to the second floor were another bedroom and a large sitting room. Both of these chambers were entered by way of the long room through what had been windows. Sarah's mother and sisters used the new bedroom as a guestroom when staying in Mendota. The sitting room on the southwest corner allowed for the maximum of light year-around where sewing, letter writing, needlework, and other activities requiring good light occurred.

The east wing of the house, an office, was constructed about 1850, but not by original builder John Muller who had drowned while working a log jam in the Mississippi River in 1845. In 1853 they would build a summer kitchen of Milwaukee brick just west of the warming kitchen. At the time, a wood lean-to on the north face of the summer kitchen covered the well, creating a space for laundry.

Not all of the upgrades that occurred after Henry and Sarah's marriage happened inside the house. Together the Sibleys built a new, spacious stone privy on the hill above their well. Though people in the 1840s just began to understand sanitation, what was understood pertained to water that could be seen, rather than groundwater. Sibley refitted one of his warehouses for an office, built a powder magazine, and made other improvements.

Completing the remodeled compound was a kitchen garden and arbor, all surrounded by a picket fence. Over the 18 years that the family resided in Mendota, periodic updates undertaken by the Sibleys continually modernized their home. They added shutters, a columned portico embracing their front entrance, and completely redecorated and refurnished the interior in 1853 upon Henry's retirement from Congress.

As far as houses go, the Sibley House in Mendota is vernacular, and probably did not have the benefit of an architect. At best one might describe the style as a side-gabled massed plan commercial building typical of pre-railroad buildings. The layout and design of the building dictated its use: form followed function. As such, the house Sarah acquired in marriage had to be reused as the layout and design allowed. The limitations on functionality, restrictions to natural light, and lack of any distinctive style probably all contributed to Sarah's desire to move to a proper house in St. Paul as soon as she could. In most ways the house was very much a working house, a starter home, and far different from the type of fine houses in which she wanted to live. (16)

Rear of Sarah Sibley's house   **Gussie – Sibley House image 1856**

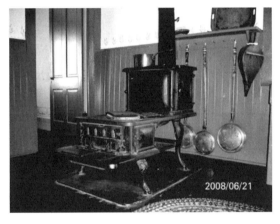

Sarah's stove

Sarah's warming kitchen
Note warming pans, like the one used
to warm Attorney General Charles
Berry's bed, December 1859.

Sarah Jane Sibley, 1858

Frederick B. Sibley

Sarah's penned words

Sarah's writing desk – closed & open

Chapter 3: Like a New Being

Sarah's own household began on May 2, 1843, when she married Henry Sibley. Unlike her example from the year before, none of her unmarried sisters, nor any of her husband's sisters, came immediately to help her. Perhaps the Sibleys felt they could manage things with the servants they had, and with the few women friends they had around Fort Snelling and the St. Peter's. Or, perhaps with both of their fathers in frail health, none of their female siblings could be spared to relocate to a remote frontier.

On June 18, 1844, Sarah gave birth to her first child, Augusta Ann Sibley, whom her parents affectionately called Guss or Gussie. Then beginning a pattern that seems to have persisted in their marriage, 18 months later Sarah delivered a son, whom they named Henry Hastings Sibley in honor of his father. However, they lost the boy in August of 1846, a day short of 8 months. The death likely underscored the need for help from female relatives.

The core strength of any family of the period remained the nuclear family of husband, wife, and children. Altogether Henry and Sarah Sibley eventually welcomed at least nine children: five boys and four girls, of whom two girls and two boys lived to adulthood. Having a large family gathered around them seems to have been an ideal for which Sarah and her husband strived. (17)

How, or if, Henry and Sarah planned their family is not known. The seasonality of their children's births is scattered with 3 in September, 2 in January, and one each in May, June, July, and August. The number of months between births is 21 to 31 for 4 of the children, 40 to 44 months for 2 more, and 60 and 18 at the extremes. Family stories suggest that Sarah had plural miscarriages, and one undated letter documents one. Women of Sarah's day both held that God was the guarantor of life who called home to heaven family members in his own good time, and that society increasingly expected women to decrease infant mortality through their diligence in caring for the family. The American character believes it can improve any situation through careful study, even infant mortality.

Some scholars suggest the difference in the firmly held belief in God as the guarantor of life and the emerging notion that women could halt infant mortality through their own efforts as two contradictory thoughts. However, the belief that Sarah held as a Christian affirms that, while God acts in history, He also gives humanity a free will – that is, even though He knows what the outcome of our choices is, this does not mean that the outcomes are foreordained. A Christian like Sarah who read and knew her Bible would ask that God open her mind so that she might quickly discover the knowledge she needed to fight infant mortality. Whether Sarah Jane ever did so, however, is unknown. (18)

Sarah's attitudes toward children evolved with her own experiences, as well as learning from broader societal thought as she aged. When Sarah began having children in 1844 she only had one close female relative in the area, namely her sister-in-law Annie Steele. Whether Annie assisted with the delivery of Gussie is not known. However, according to historian Jane Nylander, "It would have been unthinkable for her to have experienced her first delivery without a close female relative at hand." Sarah had been present for Annie's first baby, and as the years passed Sarah's sisters were on hand for the births of subsequent children. Perhaps neighbor women like Pelagie Faribault also assisted. (19)

Between the births of her first two children, Sarah's father James Steele died at age 82 on September 20, 1845, and was buried in Harrisburg. Then in April the following year, Solomon Sibley, Henry's father, died at age 77 in Detroit.

Sarah's sister Abbian Steele arrived in Mendota to help with Sarah's third pregnancy before the closing of river transportation (due to freezing) in late 1846. Abby, or Abb, as she was known, was 26 years old, and unmarried. Being closest in age to Sarah of all the Steele siblings, she and Sarah probably enjoyed a special relationship. In the few surviving letters from Sarah, Abb is most often mentioned, and most often the recipient of Sarah's intimate thoughts about her husband, children, or even underwear. (20)

Abby's stay was brief, but, along with the medical care of Dr. George F. Turner, saw her sister through the safe delivery of a second Henry Hastings Sibley whom they affectionately called "Harry." Abb married Tom Potts in her sister's parlor on October 28, 1847. Abby may have met Thomas Reed Potts, an aspiring Galena physician, on her way up the Mississippi to Mendota. Just as likely, she may have known him and his family through Presbyterian circles in southeast Pennsylvania. As three-year-old Guss Sibley was suffering from an eye malady, Abby and Tom took their niece with them back to Galena both to care for the ailment and to allow Sarah to concentrate on Harry. The Potts family would remain in Galena until 1849. (21)

Sarah Sibley presided over and managed a complex, yet all very common middle class household. Families in mid-nineteenth-century America were composed of everyone who lived in a house, whether a blood relative, visitor, boarder, or employee. Households were very fluid with people staying for varying lengths of time, or even permanently. The location of the Sibley household was not permanently in Mendota. For several months at a time the Sibleys lived in a boardinghouse while Henry was delegate in Congress in Washington City. The Sibley household was fairly typical with many comings and goings, and Sarah Jane was at the center of it all with "her executive ability and foresight." (22)

In June 1848 the household increased further with the arrival of two more of Sarah's unmarried sisters, Mary H. Steele and Rachel Elizabeth Steele, and later that fall by her mother Mary Humes Steele and never-married Aunt Elizabeth Humes. Two months later on August 26, Henry Sibley attended a meeting in Stillwater promoted as a political convention. As his biographer Rhoda Gilman describes, Sibley offered to go to Washington at his own expense as a representative to organize Minnesota Territory now that both Iowa in 1846 and Wisconsin in 1848 entered the Union. A hastily organized election in October confirmed Sibley, who hoped that the presidential election the following month would place fellow

Michigander and Democrat Lewis Cass in the White House, and make Sibley's nomination as governor of the new territory likely. Instead, Mexican War hero and Whig Party nominee Zachary Taylor became President, ending any chance of the governorship in 1849. (23)

Sarah wrote to her sister Abby in Galena in mid-September about the Stillwater convention. In reply, Tom Potts assured Henry, "Abb will write Sarah and give you all the gossip" about his family. He noted that he and Abby were invited to a wedding, but Abb would not go since she had no dress to fit her, and would not go in a "wrapper." In other words, Abb was pregnant. "Altho' Gussy complains a little of one of her eyes today, I still think they are improving," he concluded. (24)

Preparing for their departure for Washington City, Sarah wrote Abby again later in the fall. She complained that Captain M.W. Lodwick "is always in such a hurry when he comes here that he does not give me time to write any thing." She had just read Abb's letter, and was "sorry to find you were sick." Abby's first pregnancy had just started, so she was due lots of advice. "Mother says you *must* take more exercise if possible," Sarah reported, "and not stay in the house so much." Their mother was clearly worried, so Sarah counseled, "now Abb do please her if nothing else, do as she wishes." Sarah, too, was worried for her sister's health. "I begin to *smell a rat*, you dont feel so badly for nothing," Sarah wrote.

As with anyone who has lived in more than one place, Abby had asked Sarah to send some things she had left behind in Mendota. "You say send your patterns well where are they I am sure I dont know, I send some but I dont know whether they are the right ones or no." In return Sarah asked for a recipe for "spruce beer I never made it half as good as you. I want to make some and I dont know how." All the same, Sarah would "have a box ready for you by the next boat, if you do not come up, but I dont see why you cannot."

Sarah reported their sister Mary (who had just returned from a visit to Galena) and Ellen Rice had gone over to the Fort with the Capt. Ludwick of the steamer *Dr. Franklin*. Ellen Rice was the recently arrived younger sister of Henry Mower Rice and Edmund Rice. She had come west to assist her bachelor brother Henry with housekeeping. But, Sarah noted, "Miss Rice has not got at housekeeping yet." Perhaps she was having too much fun, Sarah observing that "she and Mary have great times together romping about." Ellen recalled a hunt for prairie chickens, writing that Sibley "took his wife in the only vehicle there was at Mendota, and her sister and I accompanied them on horseback." Ellen's arrival added to the society of young, unmarried women who enlivened the Fort's social scene.

Most of all, Sarah admitted of her Mother and sisters' arrival that summer to Abby, "I feel quite like a new being since they came here." Even though more of her family lived nearby, Sarah understood her new family as she "miss[ed] Mr. Sibley very much the dear good soul, kiss him for me when he arrives at Galena. Abb I love that man more and more every day I live." Then with a seeming smile wrote, "I hope you can say the same thing of the Doct, he deserves it at any rate. Give my love to him, and a smack on the lips, and write very soon." Sarah had a playful relationship with Tom Potts, noting "I received his last [letter] the good for nothing fellow. I will pay him off. I will send him one six pages long, that will fix him." (25)

Henry and Sarah left for the east on November 5, 1848 with their children Gussie and Harry, and Hercules Dousman, Alexis Bailly, Tom and Abby Potts, and Ellen Rice. Initially the group traveled by barge, playing cards and telling stories to keep their minds off the dropping temperatures and a river that was rapidly freezing over.

At the mouth of the St. Croix the party encountered the Lodwick's *Dr. Franklin*, which took them aboard on its way back up the river again to St. Paul. The stop was necessarily brief given the condition of the river. Soon all were headed to Prairie du Chien where they dropped off Dousman. The steamer continued on to the Fever River and the town of Galena. Here the Sibleys chartered a stage for Chicago and passed through the smoke of massive prairie fires lighting the night sky as far as their eyes could see. At Chicago they took passage on a steamer to cross Lake Michigan to St. Joseph, which might have been Alexis Bailly's destination as it was the place of his birth. At Niles, Ellen and the Sibleys boarded railroad cars bound for Kalamazoo, Michigan, where the party dissolved with the Sibleys continuing to the east. The trip provided Sarah Sibley with conversational fodder for years. (26)

Annie Steele preceded the Sibleys on going east to visit her Barney relatives in Georgetown. Sarah was intent on convincing her remaining brothers William, James and John in Pennsylvania to join the bulk of the family in Minnesota. That worried Frank Steele, who wrote in late November 1848 to Henry Sibley "Do not give Bill Steele any encouragement to come out." Bill inherited the milling operations along the Octoraro Creek, and with that experience, Frank did not need any additional competition for the development of the waterpower from the Falls of St. Anthony on the Mississippi. Frank hoped the Sibleys would share a house with Annie Steele while they were in Washington. "Mother and Mary are doing well a little lonesome at times but are quite happy — we are all anxious to learn the result of your election — have had no mail since the *Franklin* left." (27)

From Sarah's point of view, though, having as many of her siblings as possible come to Minnesota was desirable since her husband's work for the foreseeable future would be entwined with the new territory's development. The prospect of returning to Pennsylvania seemed as dim for Sarah as the prospect for Henry to return to Detroit.

At Strasburg, Pennsylvania, Henry left his wife and children in the care of Sarah's brother Dr. John Steele. Sarah had in mind to persuade her brother John to relocate both his family and medical practice from Strasburg to St. Paul. Sarah divided her time between the Strasburg-Lancaster area of Pennsylvania and Washington in the spring of 1849 hoping that her brothers would follow her sisters' example and come to Minnesota. While John and Catherine Steele eventually did relocate to St. Paul in 1856, the remaining two brothers did not. James married about 1857 and took up farming near Coulterville, Illinois, in the early 1860s. Bill never married but eventually moved to Illinois. On this trip in 1848-1849, Sarah only planted the idea of relocation, at least for her brother John. (28)

Three weeks later Frank again wrote to Sibley that "I wish you would see Annie as soon as possible. She is under the attendance of a Physician for a disease of the spine and of the knee joint. I do hope nothing serious is the matter. The Doctor may be a humbug and make things worse for the sake of a fee." Henry's medical experience and knowledge might have enabled him to determine the merits of the doctor's treatments, but what her ailment was is not known. (29)

Congress granted Henry Sibley a seat as Delegate in Congress, which gave hope to more than just organization of the territory. As Sarah remained in Strasburg, Pennsylvania, attempting to persuade her brother Dr. John Steele to come west, Tom Potts wrote Congressman Sibley that with a presidential appointment presumably as medical purveyor for Fort Snelling, Potts would bring Abby and their daughter Mary to Minnesota. (30)

At nearly the last moment before adjournment on March 3, 1849, Congress formally organized Minnesota Territory from the remnants of Iowa and Wisconsin. Sibley's former American Fur Company colleague and current loyal political rival Henry M. Rice had also come to Washington to help Sibley persuade Congress to create Minnesota Territory. Rice, like Frank Steele and Sibley in 1842, had also come east with the purpose of marriage. With work completed, Rice married Mathilda Whitall of Virginia on March 29. (31)

It does not seem likely that Potts, a Democrat, received his appointment from a Whig administration, but nonetheless did make "St.

Paul his permanent residence" by May 19. Tom Potts further promised in his advertisement in the new St. Paul *Pioneer* newspaper that he "will attend to all calls in his profession in town and country." As with others crowding into St. Paul trying to find any accommodation, Potts boarded in what he could find on short notice. The *Pioneer* reported, "he may be found at present, [living] at the store of Mr. W.H. Forbes." William Henry Forbes was one of Henry Sibley's trusted inner circle of fur trade clerks. (32)

With the election of a Whig administration, Sibley did not get the nomination to serve as Governor of the new territory. According to historian Theodore Blegen, though Sibley wanted the governorship, the first three Whigs that President Zachary Taylor appointed did not. His fourth nominee, the chair of the Pennsylvania Whig Party central committee, Alexander Ramsey, really wanted the collectorship of the port of Philadelphia but accepted the governorship. (33)

Ramsey would have difficulty finding "quarters for [himself] and family at St. Paul in the present crowded condition of that place," Sibley wrote him. Therefore, "it will afford me much gratification if you will come directly here, and make my house your home for any length of time that may suit your convenience. We can only promise yourself and Mrs. R. a hearty welcome, and such poor fare as the country affords."

Alexander Ramsey and his wife Anna Jenks Ramsey were from Harrisburg, Pennsylvania. The Ramseys' first house near the corner of Third and Robert in St. Paul was retrofitted from one of Sibley's fur company buildings, and was not ready for occupancy when they arrived on Sunday May 27, 1849, at 7 o'clock in the morning. As Ramsey had served as chief clerk of the Pennsylvania legislature in 1841 and had known Sarah's father James Steele, the two families made an instant connection that remained rather close over the years. So despite an offer to use a nearby St. Paul hotel room, the Ramseys stayed with the Sibleys in Mendota for six weeks.

Living with him gave Sibley an opportunity to size up the new governor and political partner. Sibley remarked to his brother Sproat that "Ramsey & his family have been with us since his arrival in Minnesota. He is much pleased with the country and the Territory is in reality advancing very rapidly." Sibley predicted the rapid advancement would make "Minnesota as a State of the Union in five or six years, and one of the very finest in it." To his brother-in-law Charlie Trowbridge, Sibley took pride that "Our Governor Ramsey takes well with the people. He is a plain unassuming man of popular manners & much good sense." (34)

During the grand Fourth of July celebration "which would have done credit to any Eastern City," Sarah and Anna further developed their friendship. At 10 o'clock that morning a glittering assemblage of "about 500 men" under the direction of Grand Marshall Franklin Steele traced a route through the new capital city. The Sixth Infantry Band from Fort Snelling led the way with dignitaries, clergy, Governor Ramsey and the territorial officers in tow. In the wake of the parade, jubilant citizens celebrated both the self-rule of the nation and their own recent right to self-rule. The parade ended at noon in what is now Rice Park, where 30 canon salvos, one for each state, saluted the republic, and echoed up the

Mississippi river gorge. After the *Declaration of Independence* was read, territorial justice Bradley B. Meeker presented a lengthy oration. Revelers adjourned to "a repast suitable to the occasion" at the recently rechristened American House, a nearby hotel under the new management of Elizabeth Parker, a transplant from New Hampshire. Parker's husband and son had remained in Connecticut while she came west – which led some to speculate idly over the situation and suggested the separation resulted from inappropriate behavior.

Teenager Rebecca Marshall missed all of the day's activities in favor of preparing herself for that evening's ball. She recalled it vividly half a century later. Despite all of the new territory's elite in attendance, she was simply struck by the entrance of Sarah Sibley, Anna Ramsey, Annie Steele, and Mathilda Rice. "I do not think four handsomer women could be found in the United States," she reminisced. "Mrs. Ramsey was easily distinguished from the others, however, on account of her regal bearing, and she immediately captured my attention to the exclusion of the others." Marshall's brother William R. Marshall, like Ramsey, was a member of the Whig Party. "Will" was also one of the evening's floor managers in charge of introducing those unknown to one another, so her recollection may have been colored by who her brother knew. However, Rebecca quickly noted that on "meeting the other three at a later date, and seeing how beautiful they were, I wondered how I could have been so partial that evening." (35)

Sarah Sibley left a remarkable impression on the early residents of the new Minnesota Territory. Her training enabled her to govern a growing household, to recruit relatives to relocate to Minnesota, and to win friends among an expanding American society in the nascent territory.

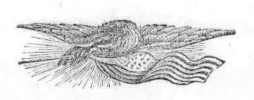

The pleasure of your company is respectfully solicited at the **GRAND ANNIVERSARY BALL,** to be given at the " Rice House" on the evening of the Fourth of July.

MANAGERS:

Dr. T. R. POTTS, *St. Paul*,	ORRIN RICE, *St. Paul*,
Dr. D. DAY, "	W. R. MARSHALL, *St. Anthony*,
S. H. DENT, "	S. NELSON, *Stillwater*,
J. R. CRITTENDEN, "	Dr. C. CARLI, "
P. K. JOHNSON, "	O. WALKER, *Marine Mills*,
B. W. LOTT, "	JOS. TAYLOR, *Falls St. Croix*,
C. P. V. LULL, "	ROBERT KENNEDY, *Prairie*,
A. L. LARPENTEUR, "	HERTZELL, *Point Douglass.*

St. Paul, *June 28, 1849.*

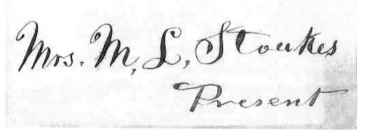

Mrs. M, L, Stoukes Present

Invitation to Grand Anniversary Ball, July 4, 1849. Teenager Rebecca Marshall remembered the entrance of Sarah Jane Sibley, along with Annie Steele, Anna Ramsey, and Mathilda Rice, at this ball.

China believed to be a wedding gift
from Henry to Sarah

Sarah's Mourning Jewelry

Lithograph. 417 Woodward, St. Paul. The house Henry & Sarah Sibley bought
July 1, 1864.

Chapter 4: Correspondents Are Sadly Remiss

Despite feeling "like a new being" with most of her family now in Minnesota, 1849 would prove to be the start of a new chapter in Sarah's life. On the one hand Sarah would be able to spend significant time with family and friends in the east, but on the other Sarah would discover the frustration of managing her household from Washington City by letter and through trusted agents. The frustration of information lag, though perhaps not new to her, must have increased to levels not known previously.

With the return of the First Infantry in August of 1849, Henry was reunited with Col. Gustavus Loomis, one of the original organizers of the St. Peter's Presbyterian Church in 1835 and an aged veteran of the War of 1812. Loomis was also a recent widower, having lost his chronically ill wife, Julia Ann, just before the regiment left St. Louis on its way north.

Despite the joy of reunion with Loomis, and the afterglow of the "Grand Anniversary Ball," a dark cloud foreshadowed events to come. "Mrs. S. has been dangerously ill within the last three days, but is now recovering," Henry mentioned to his political colleague Henry L. Moss of Stillwater. On the same day, Henry penned another letter that also mentioned Sarah's illness to his brother Fred Sibley. The purpose of that letter was to offer his youngest brother $500 per year in salary to manage the fur post while Sibley served in Washington. He assured Fred, Sarah "is convalescing." Sarah remained ill two weeks later suggesting that it was in August of 1849 that she contracted pleurisy, a viral infection of the lungs that would be exacerbated by air-borne particulates for the remainder of her life. (36)

Henry observed to his friend Captain Ned Ogden with the recently departed First Infantry now stationed at Fort Leavenworth, "the garrison ladies are not on the most cozy terms with each other." Jealousies among the ladies of Fort Snelling boiled over that fall with the arrival of newly commissioned officers fresh from West Point and the Colonel's dashing nephew, "who is quite a gallant among the ladies." (37)

With Sarah recovered from some unidentified illness of at least 18 days, throughout September and October the Sibleys made arrangements for their impending departure for Washington. Sarah ordered 7½ yards of French merino cloth, velvet trimmings of the same color, and brown-paper muslin (a stiffening material) for a new dress she would likely need during her stay in the nation's capital. Alexander Ramsey recorded in his diary four separate meetings, which likely informed Sibley of Ramsey's contacts from the two congressional terms he served in 1843-1847. The talk was not all politics, as Sarah hosted Anna Ramsey on two of those occasions. The first dinner party in Mendota included five members of the territorial legislature, plus Judge David Cooper and his wife. The second dinner was less formal and apparently included just the two couples. Ramsey accompanied the Sibleys en route to Galena aboard the *Senator*, a very slow steamer piloted by Sibley's longtime American Fur Company fellow-employee Captain Joseph Sire. They reached Prairie du Chien, Wisconsin, by 6 o'clock in the evening of November 10, after a 21-hour voyage. (38)

Sarah and her children again stayed with family and friends in southeastern Pennsylvania while Henry went on to Washington. Sarah's visit was short as Henry mentioned to his fur trade clerk and territorial legislator Martin McLeod on December 16 that "Mrs. Sibley & chicks arrived here safely and are quite well." (39)

The Sibley household in Washington resided at Eliza Peyton's boardinghouse. The boardinghouse itself took on a semblance of a household. Henry wrote his fellow housemate Dr. John B. Blake how the Sibley children "remember you and Mrs. Peyton quite vividly, and have asked sundry questions respecting you." Many residents of the boardinghouse were associated with the government, but Dr. Blake's son Edward was a student, and 11 African-Americans from age 5 to 40 were all waiters. Whether any of these blacks were enslaved is not evident from the census record. Indeed Henry and Sarah "often speak of you and the pleasant mess of which we were members, and we cherish the hope of meeting most of you once more." Despite the pleasant memories they would make in their first year at Mrs. Peyton's, the boardinghouse lacked certain amenities, such as a privy exclusively for the use of women and children. Sarah probably recalled the awkward arrangements in Prairie du Chien almost six years before when she was five months pregnant and shared a room with six men in addition to her husband. (40)

Meanwhile, back home at Fort Snelling, a near scandal ensued as the highly devout Colonel Loomis sought to replace his deceased wife. At first he gave his affections to 34-year-old Rachel Steele, but then those shifted to her older sister Mary. When Loomis came to call at the Sibley House, Tom Potts wrote, "Moll tries to get off by saying he comes to see the old lady." No one could fool Dr. Potts into believing Loomis was interested in Sarah's mother, "but it is a 'no go.' I believe she encourages the old fellow." How Sarah viewed the soap opera from Washington City probably mirrored her brother-in-law's barely contained amusement. Finding no satisfaction in either of the Steele sisters, Col. Loomis married Elizabeth Pandon of Jamaica eighteen months later in April 1851. (41)

With the loss of Loomis's attention, Rachel captured the notice of Richard W. Johnson, a recent West Point graduate from Kentucky who arrived in October 1849. She was ten years' his senior, and no doubt he was caught off-guard with his new duties, alien environment, and the swift-moving social scene of the garrison. Johnson evidently went too far in his relationship with Rachel, possibly intimating or even prematurely proposing marriage. Johnson found himself caught between his word as a gentleman and regrets of youthful rashness.

Johnson was a brevet second lieutenant, the lowest officer grade in that day, whose pay was insufficient for supporting a wife. He was also a Southerner, while the Steeles were Pennsylvanians. During the winter of 1849-1850 the sectional crisis once again reached a fever pitch, as slave owners sought to ensure that additional slave states could be created out of the land cession won from Mexico. Daniel Webster and Henry Clay, leaders from a bygone era, mustered what remained of their strength to guide Congress, which included freshman delegate Henry Sibley, through the Compromise of 1850. That compromise temporarily kept the United

States together, but Johnson's compromise in early 1850 was to postpone the marriage.

The army assigned Lt. Johnson to lead two companies from Minnesota Territory to establish what would become Fort Dodge in Iowa. His command would assist in its construction. With the marriage postponed, some of Sarah's family hoped Johnson's absence would end the relationship. Frank Steele probably found it handy in assessing the young officer that his business partner John H. Stevens would accompany the mission as the soldiers' sutler. Nevertheless, being completely infatuated, Rachel could not be dissuaded from marrying him. (42)

There is a family story that has Rachel atop the exterior stairs on the west side of the house, spyglass in hand, observing her young lieutenant at drill outside the walls of the fort. Since the environment then was an oak savannah prairie with very few trees to obscure the view, the story is plausible, but not substantiated by the historic record. However, the story does illustrate the "infatuation" Frank observed. (43)

With all of the difficulty of managing a household in two places, Sarah was glad that brother-in-law Fred Sibley arrived from Detroit in April 1850 to manage her Mendota home along with her trusted housekeeper Catherine O'Brien. Ever since he stepped off the steamboat *Nominee*, Fred found Mendota to be a challenging place. He once complained to his brother, "Please remember that while I am writing this letter, a crowd of gabbing Frenchmen & Indians are gathered in the outer room."

Fred could observe a young territory populated mostly by young families. Small children then, as at any time in history, were prone to catch ailments. Tom and Abby Potts' daughter Mary had an inflammation in her lungs, and "its fate is yet doubtful I am told" Ramsey wrote to Sibley in March. Two months later Dr. Potts reported that Mary "still has a bad cough remaining over since her attack." One midsummer day, Henry announced from Washington that "Our little Harry is very sick with an attack of Cholera inflammation. He was taken last night, and thus far remedies administered have been attended with little effect." Cholera is a bacterial infection of the intestines characterized by violent diarrhea, vomiting, muscular cramps, and collapse. But the following day, June 27, Sibley reported to his clerk Forbes that Harry was on the mend. Governor Ramsey's son Alex contracted mumps and died on Sunday July 28. The boy's funeral drew a large crowd and most of the Sibley-Steele family, but Fred admitted he "could not go being very busy here." (44)

News of little Alex Ramsey's death did not reach Henry and Sarah on the east coast until 8 days after the death. Sarah and her children, 6 year-old Guss and Harry, almost 3, had spent the summer in Strasburg, Pennsylvania. Taking advantage of recess in Congress, Henry joined them on August 4. His mail, including the news of the death of his friend's son, followed him to Pennsylvania by the 6th. Sibley returned to Washington on the 13th, and wrote his and Sarah's condolences saying they "were very much shocked to learn of the death of poor little Alex." They "grieve for you and not for him," thereby delicately showing the day's balance between submitting to God's Will, and acknowledging there was little the Ramseys could have done to prevent the death. Ramsey was thankful for their sympathy and reported that Anna and their daughter Marian were spending time in Mendota, seemingly for a change of scenery while they mourned. (45)

"I hear very little of what is going on in M[innesota]. My correspondents including Dr. Potts & Forbes are sadly remiss," Sibley had complained to Ramsey in July. Sibley's need for news stemmed from his bid for reelection as territorial delegate in Congress in the midterm elections. By the end of August, Sibley confided to Ramsey that Sarah "would be rejoiced to learn of my defeat, [and] I certainly would not shed many tears if such a result was announced." But Sibley won with 54 percent of the vote over Alexander Mitchell, a candidate fronting the schemes of Henry Rice, Sibley's most implacable political enemy. Sarah probably was justifiably proud of her husband's success, and relished the opportunity to visit her Pennsylvania relatives so frequently, but apparently disliked the abuse that accompanied a public life since Sibley claimed Sarah "would be rejoiced to learn of my defeat." (46)

Now with a full two-year term won, Sarah's mother believed the Sibleys might not return with her grandchildren on a quick visit that fall. Those fears were unfounded as Sarah could seldom be persuaded to be without the children. With all that Sibleys needed to accomplish in the four weeks they were home, however, not having to supervise them might have been preferred. (47)

Alexander Ramsey "with Dr. Potts rode up to Mendota this morning to converse with Sibley about Sioux Treaty," for which Ramsey was to be a commissioner. Sibley and Ramsey probably went over many permutations of Congressional action, and how to approach the Dakota in the event Congress approved purchasing the land of southern Minnesota. Every fur trader and Dakota had a stake in the outcome. No less was true for Sibley's colleague Joseph LaFramboise, an aged trader at Lac qui Parle. His wife made what might have been a bandolier bag for Sarah, saying Sarah "is very much obliged to her for the beautiful Bag made for her. She hopes to make some suitable return." LaFramboise likely would be satisfied just to have his debts covered in the coming treaty. (48)

When Lt. Johnson returned to Fort Snelling that fall on his way to a new assignment, his visit coincided with Henry and Sarah's brief return from Washington. What happened to convince Johnson to follow through with the marriage to Rachel Steele is unknown. Richard and Rachel were married in the parlor of the Sibley house on October 30, 1850. Sarah hosted her sister's wedding, and welcomed her mother, sisters Mary and Abby, Tom Potts, and Anna Ramsey. The entire group went to Frank and Annie Steele's in the afternoon. (49)

After an evening's amusement hosting young English adventurers Edward Whortley and Wenman Coke, who were both in their early 30s, the Sibleys departed for Washington on November 11. They left Guss and Harry in the care of family. Fred reported "As far as your family is concerned, you need be under no anxiety for I do believe that your children are in better hands than your own." Thinking better of it, Fred quickly clarified, "Of course I must not include Sarah; as I do not suppose she would agree with me if I ventured to assert that her children would be better governed than she, well cared for by her mother as by herself." Guss's chronic eye trouble continued, but Fred felt there had been a marked improvement with an application of "sweet oil." Uncle Fred who had taken to Harry, assured Sarah "They do not either of them fret after you as I supposed they would. They are very contented. And as is natural wish frequently to see you. So please confine yourselves to thinking about your children & do not indulge in any anxiety about them. Well cared for as they are by their grandmother." (50)

Letters from home helped Sarah keep current with the comings and goings at her house. Fred reported in mid-December Grandmother "Steele is now at St. Paul on a visit to Mrs. Potts, who has sent Miss Potts to comfort us in Mrs. S.'s absence." Grandmother wound up caring for her three grandchildren (Guss and Harry Sibley, and cousin Mary Potts) while the adults attended a public supper at Rev. Edward Duffield Neill's church on January 7. Neill would later go on to distinction as the chaplain for the First Minnesota Infantry during the Civil War, among other pursuits. Tom Potts joked to Henry and Sarah, "our little Mary is at your house, and the children have fine times. Everytime I get up she accosts me as Uncle Potts from hearing the other two call me so." (51)

Whatever Fred's difficulties in adjusting to his new home, by the end of the year he integrated himself with the broader family. Fred commented to his brother, "Your Detroit friends although they may approve of your resolution & judgment in leaving your children, yet certainly do predict that a certain Mrs. S. will be most monstrously lonesome without them, & I must say I do not think them more than half right." Toward the end of the letter Fred demonstrated that he felt comfortable teasing other members, suggesting to Sarah, "if you do not obtain any definite information from Miss Mary Steele, I want you to inquire of her what sort of a ride she had" with Lt. William P. Carlin for six miles up to St. Paul in a sleigh. A native of Illinois, Carlin was approximately 16 years younger than "Moll," who probably saw her sister Rachel's happiness with a much younger man as a pattern. Mary intensively dated Lt. Carlin all that winter. (52)

Mary fled Fred's teasing to the Potts's house for a respite over the holidays, followed by a longer visit to the Ramseys later that winter. Mary often stayed with friends, especially while Henry and Sarah were absent from Mendota. Fred Sibley and William Carlin were roughly the same age, making it possible that both vied for Moll's attention. Moll for her part probably welcomed attention in moderation, and seems to have kept all suitors intrigued as she did with War of 1812 veteran Gustavus Loomis. However, Loomis quickly realized that Moll, born in 1812, had no intention of agreeing to marriage. Lt. Carlin, perhaps as much as Ellen Rice (who had recently married attorney William Hollinshead), seems to have been someone Moll could safely pal around with in social settings.

Fred had other problems to deal with than to worry about Moll. With the Sibleys out of town, 18-year-old domestic servant Roselle Louvcat found herself locked out of the Sibley House late one January night. 'Rosalie,' as the family called her, had been out "visiting in the evening."

Fred wrote his brother, "It is very well that she imposed on Mrs. Steele in neglecting work &c. much more than Sarah would have allowed had she been here." The doors of the Sibley House were seldom locked at any time, so this not so subtle rebuke caused Roselle to depart "in a fit of disgust." Undaunted, sister Mary Steele asked Tom Potts to find another servant girl for the household, and to look in the nearby village of St. Anthony. Sibley's business partner and friend Hercules Dousman replaced Roselle with "a good reliable girl." Henry passed along his wife's well wishes to Jane Dousman, saying Sarah was "obliged to her for being the cause of her success in engaging" Caroline.

Without another place to stay, Roselle married her paramour Louis Lavalee on the morning of February 17, 1851. Fred reported to his brother "nearly all the Mendota world are now celebrating the festival." (53)

Conscientious help could be hard to find and retain. Unlike the comparatively brief stays of other staff, Catherine O'Brien worked for the Sibleys for several years beginning in 1850. The immature impulses of Roselle probably troubled Sarah. As Catherine was thirteen years older than Sarah, she found the steadiness of this older woman a comfort and placed a great amount of trust in her. (54)

Eighteen-hundred-fifty-one was to be a year of turning points for the Sibleys. Sarah Whipple Sproat Sibley died on January 22 in Detroit. Charlie Trowbridge, a banker and her son-in-law, handled the disposition of her estate. Fred Sibley in Mendota and Henry in Washington expressed regrets for not being with their mother in her last days. As Henry and

Sarah made their way home in spring in advance of the treaties later in the summer, Henry elected to travel on the Ohio River, rather than by railroad and through Detroit as they usually did.

As Sarah was seven and a half months pregnant, she "experienced some discomfort, but we reached home safely on the 12th" of April, Sibley explained to boardinghouse-mate Dr. John B. Blake. "Taking every thing into consideration," he continued, "we love our travelling troubles with sufficient philosophy, if not Christian patience." Sibley explained to his sister Sarah that "if I had returned by way of [Detroit] last spring, the time spent there would have passed with less pleasure than of pain." (55)

Managing family affairs from afar evidently failed in the spring of 1851. While Henry and Sarah were still in Washington City, something happened "of a sufficiently grave character" between the Sibley and Frank Steele households, "to draw from [Annie Steele] an intimation by letter that all intercourse must thenceforth cease." Even though he had since returned home to Mendota, Henry wrote to his sister-in-law Annie Steele regretting that, as head of his household, he could not visit them if their "house remains closed … to members of my own household." The matter was squarely in the hands of Sarah, who would pursue "such a course with reference to [the trouble] as her own good judgment may dictate." Whatever the situation was, it appears to have been brief yet intense. (56)

The situation may have eased also with the unifying event of birth – Sarah delivered a healthy baby girl, whom they named Sarah Jane Sibley but affectionately called "Sallie" or "Sally." Sibley, probably with a twinkle in his eye, wrote another boardinghouse-mate, Solomon D. Jacobs, that the girl "is like all new arrivals, the acme of perfection, if the judgment of the old ladies is to be looked upon as conclusive." Two months later Sibley described Sally to her Uncle Charlie Trowbridge "as fat and healthy as need be wished." (57)

The summer passed with Henry Sibley spending time working with Dakota people, his relatives, for the acceptance of a pair of treaties opening their land to white settlers. Sarah presumably tended to her household staff, renewing friendships, and spending time with her own mother, now that Henry's mother had died.

With treaties concluded, he and Sarah came to a few decisions about their accommodations for their next stay in Washington. For the second year the Sibleys decided on requiring "necessary changes being made in the arrangements of the house." To begin with, they wanted to "secure the room occupied by Judge McKinley last winter, with another adjoining." More importantly, "There should be a *privy* for the women & children exclusively, as the want of one is a serious inconvenience." Henry asked his friend Dr. Blake, a semi-permanent resident of the house, to give "us such information, as will enable me to act with a view to the comfortable location of my wife and little ones." He hoped their wishes could be accommodated as "I should prefer Mrs. P.'s to any other boarding house, as we feel more at home there than would be the case elsewhere." (58)

Chapter 5: Poor Sarah is Deeply Afflicted

"Harry is a stout, rowdy of a boy, and quite a favorite of Fred's," Sibley beamed to his sister Sarah in the summer of 1851. Sibley variously described his son as "our joy and pride," "a model of beauty," and "idol of the household." There's no question the children were at the center of Sarah's family, the focus of her attention, and that she shared her husband's sentiments. Harry figured prominently in his parents' plans for the future, perhaps taking on the family's business in time as his parents would look toward retirement.

"Stout" Harry had survived Cholera in midsummer 1850. Now a year later in late August, Harry apparently had a cold. As with many reported illnesses in the Sibley family, Henry was the primary caregiver. A few days later in September, Henry reported to his banker Charles Borup, "I had made arrangements to go down this morning to [St. Paul] but my little boy is so very unwell, that I dare not leave him." Two days later Henry wrote his former business partner Hercules Dousman that he was still "detained closely at home by the dangerous illness of our little Harry, who had an attack of inflammation of the lungs."

By September 15 he had "been for the last eight nights attending to my little Harry ... whose situation is yet a very dangerous one, although we have strong hope of his recovery." Though Henry had some training in medicine and typically cared for ill family members, Sarah no doubt shared caring for their son during his illness.

Henry was "kept at home & from sleep for more than a week." On September 17 he wrote to Borup again saying "I am used up essentially, having been with him night & day for nearly a fortnight." This sort of exhaustion could be disastrous for the health of both the ill and the caregiver. (59)

With one child very sick, and considering the children's spiritual welfare, the Sibleys had Sally baptized on Friday September 19, three months and three weeks after her birth.

"In the silent watches" early in the morning of September 20, Harry "broke out suddenly with an air and words of the little hymn *There is a happy land, Far, far away, where saints in glory stand, In bright array.*" His parents heard him recite "the prayers which he had been instructed every night to speak." A few hours later Harry died, and the grief that his parents suffered bordered on despair.

"His sudden removal has sadly deranged all my plans for the future," Henry lamented to his brother Capt. Sproat Sibley. The death made Henry "feel, that but for those of my family who remain behind, I should be willing to be laid by his side in the grave." This was the second son that he and Sarah buried. "He was so much the object of my hopes for the future, that all my plans had reference, in one way or other, to him, and I had to picture to myself his growth from mere childhood through various gradations to the stature of a full-grown man." Henry despaired to his sister Sarah A. Sibley, "I feel that one half of the life within me has been buried with my little boy."

"Our household is very sad & desolate just now," Henry admitted to Detroit physician George E. Hand. "He is missed by us all every hour in the day," Henry told his sister Sarah A. Sibley. "He was almost idolized by every one round." Harry's parents knew him to bring joy to "all who were brought in contact with him."

Henry was deeply concerned for his wife's health as she "has been seriously affected by the death of her child." Henry marveled that "she has borne herself during the tremendous ordeal she has been called upon to pass through, with more calmness & resignation than I could have hoped for." Perhaps Sarah wrote her poem, "The Sweet Briar," reflecting on "the storms of life" as a "waste behind us and before." In the poem Sarah references a "four leaved rose that I loved the best," which could be an allusion to her four-year old boy, a "flower" robbed of its scent by the "autumnal western scented wind."

Henry believed she would feel better when they all went to Washington as he had to return to Congress in a few weeks. "The change in scene will tend in some measure to dispel the deep gloom which now envelops every thing hereabouts in her mind, associated as all objects at Mendota are, with her lost child." Even so, he admitted to fellow Congressman Amos Tuck of New Hampshire, "it will be a long time before "the great restorer" will have healed the deep wound which our afflictions have received in the sudden removal of our beloved child." (60)

Sproat Sibley had married Charlotte Hart Saxton on April 12, 1851, but his brother had not acknowledged it, probably because his attention was first fixed on the treaties that summer, and then entirely consumed with Harry's sickness. "Although Sarah & I have not yet had the pleasure of meeting her, we beg you to give her our warmest love, and say we shall be most happy hereafter to greet her in person as our loved sister," Henry wrote. In closing, he assured his brother that Sarah "thinks a great deal of her brother Sproat." (61)

Sarah and Henry left for Washington, again on November 10, as they had the year before. With the death of Harry, and the departure that winter of most of the Steele women who took Grandmother Steele for one last visit to her old home, Fred observed, "I am leading a bachelor's life this winter." Although Rachel Johnson had left for the east, she returned in January 1852 as her husband was on leave from duty near San Antonio, Texas. Tom Potts, equaling his in-laws' well-honed Steele humor, quipped to Sibley, "Rach and Johnson are as *sweet* on each other as usual, much kissing and cooing, but no *apparent* result from it yet." The Johnsons wanted to be parents. (62)

Sarah was able to write a pair of letters from Washington that winter, one in January and the other on February 1, that now reside in the Livingston Papers at the Ramsey County Historical Society.

"Well what do you think of it by this time?" Sarah asked Abby, referring to Abby's new son, Henry Sibley Potts. "It is not the thing it is cracked up to be is it? Oh how I would love to see you to teaze you a little but never mind next Spring will be time enough." She had received a long letter two days earlier from Tom Potts, and "I was really delighted to hear that you got along so well with the use of Chloroform" to ease the pain of childbirth. "Abb who is it like? I want to see it so badly. Is it cross, do you lose your rest at night any?"

Sarah had spent the holidays in Pennsylvania with her brother John, whose young son James Steele was still bedridden. And, having just arrived the week before, they "have not been at any partys or Assemblys yet — and do not intend to go to any this winter." On the other hand, sister-in-law "Anne attends all is as gay as she can be her mourning attire." Sarah thought it improper that "she dances the Polka — and every other thing — her head is completely filled with the parties and the beaux like any young girl of fifteen."

Not to be outdone by other ladies in the same boardinghouse, Sarah "went out yesterday and got myself a silk — it is a green brocade with a broad satin stripe and a narrow white one. I think it very handsome — green is the fashionable color." She shrewdly "paid 2$ 12 ½ a yd" even though the clerk "asked 2.50 for it but I would not give it. Everything is so high here that I will make very few things do me."

"I left Lancaster a week ago, have been there three weeks with Abb Frazier," Sarah informed her sister. Abb was the wife of Reah Frazer, who had been a successful lawyer in Lancaster. Abbiann, born in 1827, seems to be a Humes relative, perhaps a cousin of Sarah and her siblings. Reah and Abby had four children. Reah, now 48, had recently been committed to an institution for insanity. "Indeed Abb you must write to her she feels very much hurt. I told her you intended to write very soon. She thinks you have forgotten her or dont care for her, the tears come to her eyes whenever she talks about you." Abby Potts was not the most faithful correspondent even to her own sister: "I think you ought to be ashamed for not writing to me once."

Turning her attention to Tom Potts, Sarah replied to him in February that she "hesitated some time about answering that little note of yours. I thought you might have written on botten paper at any rate." She had also been waiting on the mail for word from any of her Minnesota friends. "I have not heard from Mother or Mary for some time," but "Mary was in Harrisburg two weeks ago, where she is now is more than I can tell, she says she wishes to return home quite early in the Spring," as it "would be much more pleasant to travel than in the heat of summer." Comfort would be a factor with "the older the baby" Sally had become. "Although she is a very good child now, could not wish a better, what will Abby think when I tell her she has been eating chicken and turkey bones for the last two months, sets alone and has even learnt to slap her Mother."

Sally certainly had grown fast. "I had her vaccinated a week ago and her arm is now quite inflamed — there is always more or less Smallpox in this city so we thought we had better be on the safe side." As opposed to her daughter, her husband "has not been at all well for the last week, he took a severe cold, with fever — he is much better now but not entirely well."

"The weather here has been so very unpleasant all winter," Sarah observed, "that I wonder we have not all been sick. I am more sick and tired of Washington than I was in my life." It wasn't entirely the weather that made Sarah disgusted. "*Our* sister Anne is still flourishing. She went to the last Assembly looking more like one of these *tumble balls* than a human being. Several persons asked me if my brother was with her. I told them no, that if he was in town she would not have been there. They said they thought he would not let her make such a display. I really feel mortified when I have to tell strangers that she is my sister-in-law."

Tom Potts' colleague, and post physician for Fort Snelling, Maj. Robert Cooke Wood, was in Washington, "but how long he will remain I dont know for I think he will see enough of the Barney family in a day or two."

Still annoyed with the lack of mail, Sarah had to ask, "What is that wife of yours about? I think she is one of the laziest things that ever drew breath, and that Mrs. Johnson not much better. This is the last letter I am going to write."

When Catherine O'Brien discovered some of her mistress' spoons were missing, Fred wrote Henry and Sarah about it. Sarah set the record straight to Potts, "I have them with me and I told Fred before I left that I was taking them, [and] to let Catherine know." Somewhere communication failed, but Sarah easily managed to straighten out the problem. The distance between mistress and servant presented additional challenges.

Sarah had been in touch with Tom's elderly Mother. "She was quite an invalid when she wrote, had not been out of the house for some time." As for her own children, "Gussy is very well, has not had one symptom of the old disease. I find she is very near sighted and I suppose will be all her life time."

Territorial legislators Henry Moss and Hugh Tyler had been there "the other evening, sat about an hour or two. I find Mr. T. is not quite so friendly and sociable with me as when we were all at Mendota." Sarah preferred to be friends with all of her husband's friends, and to be treated accordingly. "I have seen him but three times this winter. I dont know but I think he called then to see Mr. S. and not me. I dont like such acquaintances. Mr. S. scolds me very much for saying so but I dont care." (63)

Sibley demonstrated his strength to numerous people and even fought with several men. He seems to have had a temper that could be set off easily. Though Sarah may have triggered that temper, there is no evidence to suggest physical violence. While it is hard to characterize Henry's scolding of Sarah in the few remaining sources, the frequency and severity certainly suggests more than occasional marital squabbles. Sarah's petulant, if defiant, assertion to Tom Potts might be understood as either sour grapes from a lost argument or standing her ground with a bully.

Meanwhile, back in Minnesota, Fred observed the territory being on the verge of a change – if only the treaties would be ratified by the Senate. He told Joseph LaFrambois, "I have been informed the Steamer Tiger starts tomorrow for the Blue Earth River (as an exploratory expedition I suppose.)" The 100-foot long *Tiger* was small enough to negotiate the irregular Minnesota River. Capt. Barton took Parsons King Johnson, Henry Jackson, and others from St. Paul to look for a suitable townsite that would become Mankato.

Fred, as with others in Minnesota Territory, implemented changes in food. That spring he ordered from Henry McCloskey, the Sibleys' grocer in Galena, almost 15 pounds of seeds for the kitchen garden: rutabaga, cucumber, long orange carrot, large yellow Altingham carrot, large red onion, long blood beet, yellow field pumpkin, nutmeg melons, muskmelons, watermelons, parsnip, early York cabbage, large late drumhead cabbage, red Dutch cabbage, late white flat turnip, and large red smooth tomatoes. The produce of the garden could be stored through the winter in one of the larders in the basement. One new item that Fred Sibley ordered for Jean-Baptiste Faribault was "12 Apple Trees of larger size. Col. Dousman, he says, procured some at Galena, which bore the same year as they were transplanted." Sarah and her family would enjoy much of the produce over the next winter. (64).

Rachel and Richard Johnson left for Texas in early April. The Steele Family hiatus in the east ended on June 27 after more than 6 months, as Ramsey reported "about noon the steamer *Ben Campbell* came in with the mail. Passengers carried up on her at one dol. per head." The high price for passage reflected the luxury of this 50-stateroom, brand new vessel for the American Fur Company's Dubuque & Minnesota Packet business. "Mary Steele & her mother came upon this boat." (65)

Rachel, homesick and writing from a camp on the Llano River, northwest of present day Austin, dreamily imagined life in Mendota to her sister Mary, "Gussy and Sally playing round the steps and Mr. Sibley "kicking up his heels" through the yard. Sarah and you sitting in the door and Mother in a chair in the hall and I even imagine that you are sometimes talking of me away here in Texas." Rachel was now over a month pregnant – the "apparent" results Tom Potts awaited over winter – and probably realized that like Sarah, none of her sisters would be present when she would deliver. "O dear O dear," she wrote, "How I wish I could see you all once more." (66)

Henry and Sarah arrived home on Wednesday September 20, 1852. He assisted Ramsey with treaty payments on October 24: "Sibley came in last night & remained here & breakfasted with us." Ramsey "finished with [Sibley's] assistance the count of gold $100,000, found it all correct." The following day Anna Ramsey hosted Sarah Sibley, Abby and Tom Potts, and Mary Steele for tea, while Sibley attended to more of the treaty business. (67)

As Sibley would not seek another term as delegate, Henry and Sarah decided he alone would go to Washington for his last session in Congress. First, however, he had business to attend to at the Prairie, as Prairie du Chien was often called. Sarah saw her husband off from St. Paul, and Fred arranged for transportation back to Mendota for Sarah and the children. Fred instructed banker Charles Borup, "do me the favor to see that the driver is a careful one." On November 19 he confirmed "Mrs. Sibley arrived safely with family – with many thanks to yourself & Dufert," the driver. (68)

The presidential election in the fall of 1852 brought New Hampshire Democrat Franklin Pierce to the White House in a landslide over perennial Whig candidate General Winfield Scott. With the change in administration, Ramsey lost his appointment as governor to a Democrat through the patronage system. Sibley probably hoped that the governorship might be offered to him. Sibley's inveterate enemy in the infant Democratic Party in Minnesota, Henry M. Rice, became delegate.

Shortly before he left for his lame-duck session, he wrote to his friend Borup, "I cannot take Mrs. S. & family with me, but as you must leave early in February for N.Y., perhaps I can so far trespass on your kindness so to ask you to take charge of her to that City where I can meet you." If he would, Sarah "will leave her children behind." The trip was important as Sibley wanted Sarah to "be able to avail herself of an offer to have her teeth attended to by a N.Y. dentist, which is the kind of reason for her trip this winter." (69) Sarah probably had her teeth attended to in the east as she seems to be conspicuously absent from parties hosted by the Ramseys in January.

She was home by late February when Fred cautioned his brother, "Sarah got all your letters care of McCloskey & says you scolded her considerably." She "was rather in the blues for a time." Sarah triggered Henry's temper again, this time by continuing to voice concerns he considered settled. (70)

All the same, Sarah loved her husband as much in 1853 as in 1848 when she had written her sister Abby that she loved him more each day. The scolding did not inhibit her girlish enthusiasm to see him that spring when Sibley was expected in Galena on April 20. When her husband began his homeward trip, like a newlywed Sarah went "down on *Excelsior*, expecting to meet my brother at Galena," Fred Sibley wrote to Henry McCloskey. Sarah's behavior, in light of her depression following this scolding, also suggests a measure of codependence, an ugly form of love wherein one spouse only sees self-worth through the other. (71)

Retirement agreed with Sibley, who confessed to his supplier in the fur trade, Pierre Chouteau Jr. & Company, "I have been to St. Paul but once since my arrival" the week before. "I find occupation at home." The optimism of opening a new territory for settlement induced Sarah to try her hand at new things. Sibley thanked Hercules Dousman saying Sarah "is very much obliged to Mrs. Dousman for the very acceptable present of fruit trees, which have come safely to hand." Perhaps with additional time he now had in retirement, Sibley could cultivate these trees. The Sibleys and Faribaults both experimented with growing fruit trees, but none seem to have survived Minnesota's winters. (72)

While Sibley's retirement from politics was intentional, Ramsey's was not. Willis Arnold Gorman, along with his family, had arrived in St. Paul in early May to assume the governorship. Ramsey recorded that Anna "had numerous calls" as the public thanked the Ramseys for four years of able guidance. And, after a four-day rainstorm in late May, Henry took his family "to ride, for the first time, this afternoon in the carriage." His occupation at home was to prepare the family and home for a major redecoration. Sarah still wanted to move into St. Paul, especially now that both the fur trade at Mendota was coming to an end and Sibley was now retired from the Delegacy. Sibley probably had strong attachments to Mendota where he had lived since 1834, but for Sarah the social life she wanted was in St.

Paul, not in Mendota. (73)

They compromised by updating the house in Mendota to be more like those in St. Paul that Sarah admired. The ideal of the day was to purchase everything at once so that all of the furnishings would match. Contemporaries of the Sibleys found inspiration for decorating by visiting commercial parlors in hotels, steamboats, and photography studios. Henry and Sarah had ample opportunity to do the same through frequent trips to Washington City and lengthy stays in that city. Much of what the Sibleys ordered was for their parlor, a formal showcase room for entertaining visitors that could demonstrate their educated taste. They bought a three-foot square walnut table for the center of the room to provide a focal point and the location of, typically, a kerosene lamp to provide light to the whole space. A new mirror would brighten and enlarge the room. A reed-bottom walnut rocking chair provided Sibley with a comfortable place to relax and read. For the Great Hall, dozens of reed-bottomed chairs were available for visitors during large parties. Henry and Sarah also ordered three new beds, two wash stands with pitchers and bowls, and six 14-inch foot tubs. New carpets throughout the house would cut down on wintry drafts. Everything came from Henry McCloskey in Galena. "Many thanks for the trouble taken by you in selecting the furniture," Sibley wrote just eight days after placing his order. (74)

Despite the improvement in her accommodations, Sarah could not entertain or go on visits as she was pregnant again. Henry informed his former colleague, Congressman Benjamin C. Eastman, "my *family* is not in a condition to leave home just now." Eastman was in St. Paul on a visit and wanted to see his old colleague. If Eastman wanted to visit, he would have to come up to Mendota. Despite the impending arrival of his child, Sibley planned to depart for New York and Washington the next day. He thought he would return in 20 days, which in some minds probably was cutting things close. Just in case he was not back in time, Sibley had Borup send chloroform to Mendota "by the first opportunity." As it was, he did get to visit with Eastman as both departed aboard the *Nominee* from St. Paul at 10 o'clock Sunday morning. (75)

Sibley returned in early July, and as he prepared for the arrival of another child, he also had to prepare for the departure of his beloved younger brother Fred whose three-year contract with the fur company was ending. After Fred's first year, Sibley had confided to brother-in-law Charlie Adams, in Detroit, "Fred is troubled with the blues to-day, and not without reason, for our last year's business is few [on account] his affairs to turn out a losing one." Sibley regretted having persuaded him to come to Mendota and enter the trade, "but of course I did it with the belief that it could all turn out to his benefit." With the death of their mother Sarah Whipple Sproat Sibley, Fred inherited an interest in a quarry. While Fred missed his mother who really did not want him to go to Minnesota, the death of his nephew Harry Sibley on September 20, 1851, further added to a need for a change. Fred appears to have confided to few in 1853 that he would make a change. Sibley responded tersely to Joseph LaFrambois that "my brother Fred has gone on a visit to Detroit. I do not understand your allusion to his 'new adventure.' He has undertaken none that I know of." Once the news broke, on July 15 Sibley wrote to the company "My brother having declined according to the terms of our arrangement last winter, his interest in the Northern [Outfit] closed on the 1st inst. with the expiration of O. 1853." Fred would not immediately leave, "but will devote his time for a few months assisting me in bringing matters to a conclusion." (76)

As time grew closer for Sarah to give birth, Sibley, who had once again been up much of the night into Monday morning, August 1, wrote his former partner Hercules Dousman, "Can you not secure a good Norwegian girl for us some time this month?" Sarah would need additional help after she gave birth. A little later in the morning Sibley wrote to his friend entrepreneur William Gates LeDuc in Hastings that Sarah "presented me with a fine boy this morning." Sarah named him for her brother, Franklin Steele Sibley. (77)

Sarah's bed

Sarah's wardrobe

Sarah's birdcage
Believed to be a gift from a Dakota woman.

Sarah's sewing table
Gift of Sandy Elmstrom

Chapter 6: Difficult Getting to St. Paul

In 1933, Master's degree candidate Ellsworth Carlstedt analyzed Minnesota's explosive growth during the five years between Henry Sibley's retirement as Delegate in Congress and its admission as a state. In the decade prior to statehood, Sarah and her relatives had contributed to the white population increase of 3,322 percent. Additionally, while 212,000 acres sold in Minnesota between 1848 and 1853, over the next 4 years 5,250,153 acres sold. No other state had as intense a growth spurt as Minnesota and Sarah looked to take advantage of the expanding social scene. (78)

Sarah Sibley settled back into the society of early Minnesota in the fall of 1853. Two year-old daughter Sally had dysentery for a little over three weeks, but was "convalescing" by October 22. She was well enough to permit Alexander Ramsey to find "Mr. & Mrs. Sibley dining with us" at 1:30 on the afternoon of October 26. Sally's illness unhappily brought to mind their son Harry's death in 1851. (79)

Captain Robert Granger wrote to the Sibleys from Fort Mason in Texas with praise for their brother-in-law Lt. Richard Johnson. Granger had been at Fort Snelling with the First Infantry in the late 1830s, along with Gustavus Loomis and Ned Ogden. "I am glad to learn that Johnson is held in such high estimation among you," Sibley replied. "His wife is really a fine woman." (80)

Six Miles from St. Paul

Their retirement from politics left the Sibleys time to correspond with their many friends. Sibley regaled his readers with the facts of a Minnesota winter in January 1854. "The snow is two feet deep and the deer too poor to kill. Consequently I shall let them alone for this season," wrote Sibley, a well-known hunter, to Congressman Ben Eastman. "The weather is very cold, so much so that sleigh riding is not as pleasant at it will be by & by," he told former boardinghouse-mate Dr. Blake.

Getting to St. Paul could be problematic. "I am anxious to have a good road from this point [Mendota] to St. P. on this side of the Miss.[issippi] and this can only be done if a regular ferry is kept up," Henry Sibley had written to his friend Alexander Ramsey in 1851. Crossing rivers and traversing the irregular bluffs all took time. At least now with the cold weather "and the ice on the Mississippi being firm we can readily reach the Capital in half an hour from Mendota, so that we can have as much company as we desire." Except, Sibley could have added, in cases of illness, as he wrote the same day to Borup, "I fear I shall not be able to call down to-morrow, as I am not well." He had glandular swelling in his throat and shoulder, so "I fear the effects of cold." The distance from Mendota prohibited easy access to St. Paul and to have company as often as Sarah desired. (81)

Indeed the isolation of Mendota during the Minnesota boom became pronounced. Just 6 days after declaring they could have as much company as they desired, Sibley lamented to Henry Rice in Congress, "Things are dull here, ... and the country manifests little life, in consequence of the deep snows and continued cold weather." And company became even thinner when his brother Fred Sibley left on February 10. "We shall miss him much," Sibley told fur trader Norman W. Kittson. (82)

As Fred returned to Detroit, Henry and Sarah looked forward to receiving a visit from his sister Sarah Augustine Sibley. In the summer of 1851, Sibley wrote a long letter to her pleading with her to come to Minnesota for the summer. "The country is so beautiful," he wrote trying to entice her to come. "Everything wears an air of so much freshness and novelty, that a residence of even a few months here, would set like a charm upon you, and add years to your life." Perhaps he hoped his single sister might find a husband as his wife Sarah and her sisters Abby and Rachel had all done. He assured her that "opportunities are constantly presenting themselves" to come west, as on February 22, 1854, an all-rail connection from Chicago to Rock Island on the Mississippi River opened, enabling Americans to travel from New York via Chicago to the Mississippi River in just two days. The new rail fueled an economic boom in the Upper Midwest, as did the so-called "Grand Excursion of 1854" that brought eastern capitalists to see potential western investments. The Grand Excursion arrived in St. Paul quite unexpectedly early on June 8, 1854, the same day Sibley wrote that he and Sarah "hope to see you & madam up here with the great party" to his grocer Henry McCloskey. (83)

Sarah A. Sibley arrived in Mendota on June 12, and must have seen at least some of the flotilla of steamers on their return trip downstream. She had not traveled the new rail route, but instead had taken the stage from Chicago to Galena as the Sibley family had often done while Henry was in Congress. "I feel very grateful for your kindness and attention, and that of Mrs. McC. to her, while she was in your City," Sibley thanked McCloskey. (84)

Sarah A. Sibley's visit was short, though her brother did everything he could think of to convince her to stay. "I have taken Sarah around to see the beauties of the country," he wrote Fred. "She is delighted of course she would be. I regret she is to make so short a visit, but Charlie Adams has frightened her about the Cholera." Sibley's brother-in-law and confidant Charlie Trowbridge considered making a visit also. On the eve of Independence Day when a visit from Trowbridge seemed unlikely, Sibley speculated "perhaps we may have turn to pay you all a visit by & by" instead. As for what it was like in Mendota, his sister "Sarah will be able to give you a better idea of Minnesota than I can." (85)

The next family visitor was Tom Potts' mother, who arrived from Philadelphia. "Tell Abby not to put herself out for us, as we are plain, and will give as little trouble as possible," she wrote her son. Despite warnings to the contrary, fellow ex-Pennsylvanians made her visit memorable, even if it was a bit fussy. Her fellow Pennsylvanian Alexander Ramsey played host. He rented two horses and a carriage to drive her to St. Anthony one day, and four days later held a dinner party for her and a number of others. Sarah Jane and her sisters spent time with the senior Mrs. Potts who remembered them all fondly in a later letter to her son. (86)

Sarah Jane Sibley hosted Anna Ramsey, daughter Marian Ramsey, and Marian's nurse for five days in November. Alexander Ramsey complained that he caught a cold on the way back to St. Paul after dropping his family in Mendota. The firm foundation of Sarah's friendship with Anna Ramsey, developed since the Ramseys lived with the Sibleys in May and June 1849, enabled Anna to pay frequent visits to Sarah. (87)

1854 closed "cold but clear & delightful. There is not enough snow on hand for good sleighing," Sibley remarked to McCloskey on Christmas Day. When Alexander Ramsey returned from a trip to Pennsylvania and Washington in February, Henry and Sarah dinned with the Ramseys to catch up on the news. (88)

Sarah's unmarried Aunt Elizabeth Humes' health began to sag. "I doubt whether she will long survive," Sibley told "Aunt Betsy's" nephew Frank Steele. On February 18, the doctor had drained an astonishing 3 gallons of fluid from her to relieve dropsy, which is an abnormal accumulation of fluid in the intercellular tissue spaces or body cavities. Aunt Betsy rallied, but seemed to stay close to home for the remainder of the year. (89)

As the year wore on Sarah vented to her husband that territorial Judge Andrew G. Chatfield had not called on her when he was in to St. Paul at the end of March. People bypassed Mendota more and more as they traveled about the bustling territory, which reinforced Sarah's desire to be in St. Paul where she might have a chance of seeing friends. Sibley himself summed it up a few days later to his friend Hercules Dousman, "Things [are] dull enough up here." (90)

Sibley remarked "no news" and "nothing new" in correspondence that spring. Sarah's brother Frank Steele, his wife Annie and their children had returned, but Sarah and Henry "have not seen them." When Anna Ramsey arrived for a day visit on Thursday June 28, bad luck accompanied the trip as her husband wrote with frustration in his diary, "broke tongue of carriage."

The Sibleys had not been terribly active on the social scene because Sarah was pregnant again. Mary Steele Sibley was born on September 22, 1855. Her proud parents affectionately called her "Mamie" to distinguish her from the other Marys in the family. (91)

In the New Year, Alexander Ramsey took Anna up to Fort Snelling to call upon the officers of the garrison and invite them for a party the following Thursday. While they were in the neighborhood, they stopped at Mendota and dined with Sarah and Henry. The Ramseys appear to be among the few regular visitors to Mendota. The old fur post must have seemed quite desolate. The fur trade had moved farther west with the line of settlement. Those still engaged in the business regularly wintered at more remote posts, returning to Mendota in the warmer months, as the Faribault family had done for two generations. Jean-Baptiste Faribault's wintering post had been at the Little Rapids on the Minnesota River near present-day Chaska, and his son Alexander wintered on the Cannon River where the present City of Faribault stands. But, with Sibley's involvement in the fur trade coming to an end, those still engaged had less reason to come to Mendota.

United States Senator James Shields from Illinois lost his bid for reelection in 1855. While Delegate from Minnesota Territory, Sibley knew and worked with Shields. Shields worked with another friend of Sibley's, Senator Stephen A. Douglas, on the passage of the treaties of Mendota and Traverse des Sioux in 1851. Three years later, Douglas' gambit of "popular sovereignty" in the Kansas-Nebraska Act of 1854 left Shields politically vulnerable. Many considered the Kansas-Nebraska Act as a disguise for extending slavery to territories, thus when those in Illinois opposed to slavery gained a majority in the Illinois legislature, they struck at Douglas' lieutenant.

One of the new legislators was Abraham Lincoln, who immediately, upon election to the Illinois House of Representatives, declared himself a candidate for senate. The initial vote had Lincoln with a slim margin over Shields, and a small number for Lyman Trumbull. After nine ballots, where along the way Shields was dropped by the Democrats in favor of Governor Joel Matteson, Lincoln acquiesced to Trumbull to ensure the Senate would not remain in Democratic hands. To salve his defeat, the Pierce Administration gave Shields a commission with the federal land office and sent him to administer claims in Minnesota for half-breeds, the descendants of inter-racial marriages between Anglos and Dakotas. (92)

James Shields suffered from a cold that January day when he arrived in Mendota looking for Alexander Faribault. Shields partnered with Faribault to develop Faribault's wintering post into a city. "As my cold continued to grow worse," Shields told his friend, newspaper editor Daniel A. Robertson, "Mr. Sibley urged it with great earnestness I remained his guest until Friday. I am very glad now I did so as Mrs. Sibley began to think there must be some very shady reason for my manner of passing without ever consenting to stay." Like Judge Chatfield, Shields, whom Sarah knew from her time in Washington, had not stopped to visit.

"They made my visit very pleasant. Did everything in the world to render it agreeable &c.," Shields wrote. Then turning to the rift in the nascent Democratic Party between the Sibley-Steele plurality and Henry Rice's supporters, Shields wrote that "we talked some of the coolness between you and them. I took the liberty of urging that their past feuds should end." Robertson was a man of science and authored papers on astronomy, ethnology, horticulture and phrenology. He also edited the *Minnesota Democrat* newspaper, the political voice of Henry M. Rice. With Rice now delegate, and a Pierce Administration, Robertson had also wanted to be appointed Minnesota Territory governor as did Sibley. Shields' description of "coolness" was an understatement.

But to begin to heal the division among Democrats in Minnesota, Shields needed to start somewhere. "Mrs. Sibley said every thing in the kindest spirit about Mrs. Robertson. Said she knew she was one of the first ladies in the territory, that every one said so and that her acquaintance would be an acquisition." Perhaps the two cultured women, Sarah Jane Sibley and Julia Robertson, could cement a friendship whereby Sibley and Robertson could also work together.

Shields continued, "But evidently they think you, though a man of talents, character and energy, a soul of implacable spirit." The Sibleys were stung by Robertson's vigorous support of Rice through misleading statements about Henry Sibley. Shields believed Robertson did so with "a heart as kind and tender as that of a child behind it."

Shields had been too ill to attend the Ramseys' party on January 17, 1856, and had remained at the Sibley House in Mendota. However, he reported to Robertson, who had been at the party, that Sibley raved during breakfast the following morning: "Mrs. Robertson was the most beautiful and elegant lady at the party" of approximately 250 people. With a smirk Sarah "laughingly made him except his wife," as she had also been at the party. (93)

Time would tell if Sibley and Robertson might mend their relationship through Shields' efforts, and possibly through Julia and Sarah.

Although Aunt Betsy Humes, the never-married sister of Sarah's mother, had survived her health crisis the year before, she succumbed in early February 1856. Alexander Ramsey attended her funeral on the 8th, which was also Sarah Jane Sibley's 33rd birthday. Ramsey remarked warmly in his diary that "Miss Elizabeth Humes [was] familiarly called 'Aunt Betsy.'" Betsy's remains are interred in the Sibley plot at Oakland Cemetery in St. Paul. (94)

"This is my first lonely Sunday, four long days have passed since you took your departure," Sarah wrote her husband on March 2, 1856. "I endeavored to shorten one by going to St. Paul – I took Guss with me and had her likeness taken – a pretty good one I think." Going to St. Paul continued to be a focus for Sarah, as that was where culture and material goods to ease life could be found.

Six Miles from St. Paul

"To day there were just six of us at Church rather a small congregation dont you think? We are to have no preaching on next Sunday," at the non-denominational Protestant church her husband had constructed in Mendota in 1854. Sarah Jane's "Mother is at St. Paul, Mary at home – everything goes pretty much as when you left" Another reason to move to St. Paul was that "The soldiers have been a little troublesome at night threatening to tear down those grog shops above us" in Mendota. But she reassured her husband, "I believe there was a guard sent over last night so it was much more quiet."

Henry Sibley had an operating farm and employed John Shields (who does not seem to be related to James Shields), who "was taken sick last night." Brother-in-law Dr. Thomas Potts arrived to see Shields as Sarah was in the process of writing her letter and "had a great long string of something to tell you about" territorial governor Willis A. Gorman and some others in St. Paul. Not having the patience to decipher what Tom was trying to say or the significance of it, she "told him just to take a piece of paper and write it himself. If every thing is true what he says, I must confess there is a great deal of consistency in some of their doings." Sarah Jane's importance to Henry's political career was essential. Just as she was asked to repair the political relationship of Henry Sibley and Daniel Robertson, Sarah now understood "a call I had" from Maria Acker Rice, the wife of Edmund Rice and sister-in-law of Henry M. Rice. Ever the savvy politician herself, she laughingly wrote, "I strongly suspect you have a finger in the pie, if so you can afford to bring a lot more pretty things from New York."

In closing she pined, "Oh how I wish you were at home once more but I must wait patiently." Tom Potts, since he would be returning to St. Paul, could take her letter so that it might go out in Monday's mail. With a smile she closed "hoping you dream of me nightly I remain your true and loving wife." (94)

The explosive growth in Minnesota's population and humming economy must have finally convinced Sarah Jane's brother, Dr. John Steele, to join the bulk of his siblings in Minnesota. However, joining the crowd when demand is highest can also be difficult. "I have purchased a good, convenient house for you in this place, for which I have agreed to pay $2,000 in cash," Henry wrote his brother-in-law. Nearly 2,800 parcels of St. Paul property sold in 1856, which probably made this the worst possible year in the 1850s to buy property. "The property is a good one and you can sell it at anytime for $3,000 if it does not suit you. I will send you a full description of the property in a day or two. It is in the lower town, not very far from Potts!" Lowertown is that part of St. Paul between Jackson Street and Trout Creek, which flows between downtown St. Paul and Dayton's Bluff to the Mississippi River. In the 1850s-1860s Lowertown was the main residential district with more than 60 blocks of houses. Still, housing was tight during the real estate boom in St. Paul. Henry "could not rent a house for [John Steele] on any terms after having been disappointed in one instance." (96)

Dr. John Steele was 47 years old in the summer of 1856. His wife, Catherine McClung Steele, 45, was mother to their four children James,

Elizabeth, Mary, and Charles. Sarah had spent much time while her husband served in Congress attempting to persuade her brother to come to St. Paul. His 15-year-old son James had been chronically ill, and bedridden during recent years. Perhaps advertisements for Minnesota declaring the "salubrious" effects of its weather on health also convinced John to move his family. Sarah must have been overjoyed that he finally decided to come. She probably also wished she could join him and her sister Abby Potts in St. Paul. (97)

Anna Ramsey again paid Sarah a visit on August 26 when her husband attended a meeting at the Sibley house. The Board of Regents for the University of Minnesota met around the Sibley's dining room table to decide on building classrooms. The University had been founded in 1851, received land from Frank Steele in St. Anthony (now Minneapolis), but had not really begun to function. Sarah's brother Franklin Steele presided, while Sibley and Alexander Ramsey served on the board of regents. Ramsey "offered a resolution that under the circumstances it would not be advisable to expend at this time over $15,000 on buildings." However, the resolution was defeated by the "casting vote of Prest. Steele." (98)

Many believed the continued glow of Minnesota's booming economy would last, as apparently Frank did during the regents' meeting. Rampant land-speculation drove prices for property to new highs; this happened to Sarah's brother Dr. John Steele. Still some were unsure the future could sustain the growth.

Six Miles from St. Paul

Throughout the late winter of 1857 Minnesotans continued to believe that there would be little disaster for the territory's economy. Congress passed a bill authorizing a land grant for railroads on February 9, and the news elated Minnesotans. "Go it! Go it!" screamed the headlines on broadsides and newspapers advertising celebratory exercises set for Thursday March 19. With railroads built, surely the territory's economy would soar to new heights. The language of the railroad bill for Minnesota required a railroad to be built from Stillwater to Breckinridge. Therefore, on March 19, over 100 people from St. Paul entered Stillwater at 3 o'clock in the afternoon behind the brass bands from Stillwater and St. Paul.

Alexander and Anna Ramsey had arrived earlier by sleigh, snow still being on the ground. "We paid a visit & remained with Capt. Holcombe," he recorded in his diary. William Holcombe and his second wife Henrietta King Holcombe engaged in lumbering and were among the leaders of Stillwater. Henry and Sarah Sibley also attended along with their bankers Charles Borup and Henry Oakes and their wives, Frank and Annie Steele, and many others. "The city presented a brilliant and magnificent appearance," Andrew J. Van Vorhes reported in his *Stillwater Messenger*. "Almost every available pane of glass was illuminated with one or more lights, while a continuous line of bonfires threw their dazzling light upon each side of Lake St. Croix for a distance of two miles."

Dancing began at 9 p.m., followed by a supper at midnight. While most returned to dancing after the meal, a "Railroad Banquet" began at 1 a.m. in the Lake House Dining Hall. There, after another meal was consumed, several leading men, including Sibley, arose to give a toast or a response. Franklin Delano, a railroad investor, offered many of the toasts, including one to the new territorial governor, Samuel Medary, who was appointed by the recently inaugurated President James Buchanan. One can imagine Sibley seated next to Sarah, arising to graciously say that "he was opposed to importing Governors ... while we have so much talent within our own borders – but if one *must* be imported, he could welcome no other with a warmer hand than Col. Sam. Medary." Ramsey must have been present, although Van Vorhes does not report him at the banquet. Given Sibley's comment, perhaps people considered Ramsey part of the talent within Minneosta's borders. Sibley's response demonstrated his long-held desire to be Governor.

No telling either what the Sibleys thought of the event, but the conviviality of the evening probably satisfied Sarah's desire for socialization. They caught up on news with distant friends and made new acquaintances. The party showed what could be accomplished culturally in larger towns, possibly further encouraging Sarah to discuss with Henry a move to St. Paul.

Anna and Alexander Ramsey left Stillwater the following morning at 10, once they recovered from the late night. "When we left," Ramsey noted, "it was snowing rapidly & continued for 2 hours. Expense of the trip in money paid out $7.00." And perhaps a harbinger of things to come, despite relocating to Minnesota's "salubrious" climate, young James Steele, the long ill son of Sarah's brother Dr. John Steele, died at age 16 in March. Minnesota's land for railroads would not solve all the looming economic problems either. (99)

Amid the exuberance of the Stillwater party, national events ratcheted the intensity of the slavery issue that Sarah Jane had witnessed while her husband was Delegate to Congress seven years before. James Buchanan took the oath of office on March 4, pledging to abide by the decision of the Supreme Court. The Court considered the case of Dred Scott, a slave of Dr. John Emerson, post physician in the 1830s at Fort Snelling. Scott and his supporters argued that Scott's presence in free territory, his marriage at Fort Snelling, and the birth of two children in free territory accrued to give him freedom. Abolitionists hoped to further erode the Fugitive Slave Act that allowed for the capture and return of escaped slaves of southern plantation owners. Although a fairly small fraction of a percent of enslaved African Americans attempted escape, and fewer succeeded, the issue became symbolic to extremists on both sides of the issue. When the Court ruled against Scott, it sent the nation into a furor that captivated the attention of Congress, excluding the consideration of a bill admitting Minnesota as a state. Henry Sibley's position is unclear beyond "noncommittal." What Sarah thought of slavery is even harder to determine without any evidence whatsoever. (100)

The early 1850s were a time of transition for Sarah's sister Rachel Johnson and her army officer husband. After his promotion to second lieutenant in the First Infantry, Richard Johnson wrote to his brother-in-law Henry Sibley, delegate to Congress. Richard had "seen the President's message – from it learn that he recommends an increase in the army."

Expanding the army meant more commissions were available for army officers who often spent decades in rank waiting for vacancies above them due to retirement or death. He pleaded to Sibley to "do all you can towards securing me a commission in one of them – the commission being of as high a grade as you can get." Johnson's promotion came slowly, and during 1853-1855, while still serving in the First Infantry, he served an appointment as Regimental Adjutant, which is similar to "chief of staff" in an army unit. On March 3, 1855, he finally received promotion to first lieutenant in the Second Cavalry, one of the newly created regiments. With promotion came better pay, but Johnson remembered in his memoirs that on reaching New Orleans, Rachel discovered she needed a whole new wardrobe since style had changed greatly during their residence at remote army posts in Texas.

Rachel wrote to Sarah in April 1857, shortly after returning to Fort Mason where they had lived in 1851 with the First Infantry. "When I get a letter from home it sets me to thinking very hard about going to see you though I suppose I will have to be satisfied with thinking until next Spring. Mr. J. talks of getting a leave of absence next fall but I think the spring would be the most pleasant season to go north as then we would escape the heat of a summer in Texas and the severity of a Northern winter," Rachel mused.

Whether Sarah was teasing or truly wondering, Rachel responded to her sister's questions, motivated by the inherent racism of the era. "You appear to think we are living a savage kind of life. Mr. J. out killing Indians and I left to take care of the little ones. It is rather a dark picture, but this does not occur every day. Mr. J. has not been on a scout since last winter." Rather, "we are living quite civilized in manners and customs, and only one hundred and thirty miles from the City of San Antonio. Still I would be quite willing to abandon it had Mr. J. the means of resigning. Two thousand a year is a very convenient little sum if it is in the Army."

Historian Susan J. Matt elaborated on the conflict for women in the 1850s that Rachel alluded to in her letter. Matt wrote, "The imperatives of the expanding capitalist economy increasingly demanded of young people … a willingness to leave home, to cope with separation, and to wait for rewards." Rachel's homesick letter from 1852 where she imagines her close relatives at ease in front of the Sibley house shows that she longed to return, but that she was resigned to making due with her husband's situation in 1857.

Richard Johnson had been promoted to captain the previous December and commanded the post. However, Rachel wrote they expected Maj. George Henry Thomas to arrive in a few weeks and relieve her husband of command so that he could return his attention to his own squadron of cavalry.

As to Abby Frazier, she lamented, "I had not heard of Col. Frazers death until I received your letter. Mary mentioned his being in the lunatic assylum. Does Abby ever write to you?" Sarah had stayed often with Reah and Abby Frazier during Henry's terms as territorial delegate in Congress during the early 1850s. Sarah probably remained as concerned for Abby as she was in 1852 when she pleaded with her sister Abby Potts to not neglect to write Abby Frazier.

Though Sarah and Henry both attended Presbyterian services, Sarah's mother had been raised Methodist. She may be the Mary Steele listed in the earliest surviving membership roll of St. Paul's Jackson Street Methodist Church. Rachel beamed in her letter to Sarah, "Tell Mother we had Methodist preaching here a short time since, something very unusual in this place. I did not attend, my servant woman was sick and I staid at home." But, "I am glad Mother can get to her church occasionally, no doubt she enjoys it very much."

After remarking on their domestic servants and the unseasonably cold weather, Rachel reported she was "busy making the childrens summer clothes, I see no end to my sewing. Dr. [Andrew Kingsbury] Smith has sent for a piano on his increase of pay. For my part I would be very well satisfied with a sewing machine."

She closed with reassurances of her health. "I dont think I am looking quite so much like a ghost as when I left you. Mr. J. and I have been told lately by several persons who had not seen me for a year that I was looking very well, but the secret of it was I had just come in from the kitchen where the heat of the stove had given me some color." (101)

The national economy crashed with demise of the Ohio Mutual Life Insurance Company in August, prompting the Panic of 1857. The disastrous effects of the Panic of 1857 were, people hoped, to be avoided by the railroad land grant. But the local impact can best be seen in the number of lots sold in St. Paul. In 1856, when Sarah's brother Dr. John Steele bought his home, almost 2,800 lots of real estate changed hands. During the entire year of 1857 only 790 lots did.

That summer the federal government took a census of the white residents of Minnesota to determine if the territory met the requirements for admission as a state. With bank, business, and personal failures rampant, and people moving on to other places as a result, the territory barely surpassed the 150,000-resident threshold needed to be admitted as a state. Statehood was expected in the fall, provided Congress approved. Therefore the state's political parties convened to nominate slates of officers.

The Whig Party, to which Alexander Ramsey had belonged, had virtually ceased to exist in the mid-1850s. The northern members of that party allied with anti-slavery men in other parties and formed the Republican Party, just ahead of the 1856 presidential election. Minnesota's Whigs cast adrift by the disintegrating national party, re-formed as the Republican Party. It met ahead of the nascent Democratic Party, and nominated Alexander Ramsey for governor on September 10. He "accepted the nom. in open convention," Ramsey recorded in his diary. Five days later he further recorded, "Democratic State Convention today nom. H.H. Sibley for Governor." Two old and dear friends now faced each other in the race for the governorship. (102)

It was a bitter contest, at least in the papers. While Sibley did not venture out to do his own campaigning, Ramsey took at least one trip through south-central Minnesota, stopping in Henderson, Arlington, and Glencoe. Campaigning for oneself was a relatively new phenomenon in the 1850s. Tabulation of the vote took a long time due to its closeness, but on December 19 Sibley wrote to his friend William LeDuc in Hastings, "The agony is over, and I am elected by the Canvassers." (103)

Sibley was now governor of a presumed state as Congress had still not passed its bill for admission. Congress delayed largely because of the sectional discord over slavery. The Compromise of 1850 ended equality in the Senate for slave and free states when California was admitted. The House of Representatives, being based on population, had long ago become dominated by the north. With Minnesota seeking admission as a free state, the free states of the north would possess now four more senators than states in the slave-holding south. In short, the Dred Scott decision was too fresh in the minds of legislators in Congress with conflicting agendas regarding the slavery issue — at least to admit Minnesota as a free state in the fall of 1857.

While the years after Sibley's term as Delegate seemed like a good opportunity to quietly settle back into Minnesota society, tumultuous national events intervened. The crush of immigration into the territory — including Sarah's brother John — offered many chances to acquire new members to Sarah's circle of friends, such as Julia Robertson. But the great numbers of people placed a high demand on property, driving up land prices and mortgages. The economic upheaval just months before statehood prevented Sarah from realizing her goal of moving into St. Paul because her family's investments in land suddenly were not as valuable. Of more concern, the national debate over slavery portended ominous things to come that few were ready to talk about. However, with the election of Henry as the first governor of the State of Minnesota, Sarah would achieve her highest position in society and have the ability to make a significant contribution of lasting importance to the state.

Henry Sibley, 1860

Sarah Sibley, late in life

Daughter, Sarah Jane "Sally" Sibley
about 1875

Daughter, Augusta Ann "Gussie" Sibley
summer 1868

Son, Henry Hastings "Harry" Sibley

Son, Franklin Steele Sibley

Chapter 7: First Lady of Minnesota

Upon statehood on May 11, 1858, Sarah Jane Sibley became Minnesota's first "First Lady." The term used in the nineteenth century for this informal office was "Governor's Wife," but it carried many of the same unofficial expectations as First Lady does today. Often, wives of men in high office exercised leadership on behalf of the public, but in subdued tones so as not to draw inappropriate attention. Sarah perhaps had a few ideas in mind as she had often commented on the appropriate behavior of others. In responding to a request to assist the Mount Vernon Ladies Association, she launched Minnesota's first historic preservation campaign. However, personal factors and forces far beyond her control would make success elusive. Her effort to raise money for preservation shows just how closely the new state was tied to national events.

Interest in historic preservation in the United State was very low as America looked toward a bright future. Thomas Jefferson, for example, thought colonial buildings reflected the nation's "architectural immaturity" – replacement was to be encouraged. During the War of 1812, however, Americans began to look for strength in the places associated with their success against Great Britain during the War for Independence. The tide of feelings welling up from the seemingly successful War of 1812 centered on patriotism. Historic preservation followed suit. In 1816 citizens saved Pennsylvania's Old State House, restyled "Independence Hall," from threatened demolition. Through the rest of the nineteenth century, successful preservation often depended on three factors: patriotism, women's leadership, and private initiative. (104)

These key factors saved Mount Vernon. In 1853 Ann Pamela Cunningham, a South Carolinian, organized the Mount Vernon Ladies Association (MVLA) to save, restore, and preserve the tomb and estate of George Washington. Slave owner John A. Washington, George's great-nephew, owned the dilapidated site and opened it to tourists. Cunningham initially organized a small group of southern women, mostly from Virginia and Georgia, to rescue the estate not only from ruin, but also from northern men "who would give that spot to the grasping hand of speculation." St. Paul *Daily Pioneer* editor and Sibley friend Earle S. Goodrich visited Mount Vernon in October 1853, and concluded, "It should brand the heart of every true American with shame, if the greatest of our benefactors is to be thus rewarded." Cunningham soon realized that northern women generally felt the same as Goodrich, and with their access to discretionary capital was needed by the MVLA. As the sectional crisis over slavery in the 1850s resisted resolution, the preservation effort for Mount Vernon took on the additional cast of a way to bind the nation together. Women claimed that their private efforts, centered on patriotism, could heal divisions created by politics.

In 1856, the group, by then called the Mount Vernon Ladies Association of the Union, gained a charter from the Virginia Assembly so that it could enter into a contract and hold title to the estate. John Washington had set the price for the mansion, tomb, outbuildings, and 200 acres at $200,000 (equivalent to $4.1 million today). The women increased their fundraising goal by an additional $300,000 ($6.25 million) for restoration and preservation costs. (105)

Cunningham then set about building her nationwide organization. She became the head, or regent, of the Mount Vernon Ladies Association. Working with a small personal staff, she appointed suitable women as vice-regents to direct fundraising in their respective states. These appointments had to be carefully made because MVLA would appoint vice regents for life. Among qualifications, "good social position and family influence cannot be dispensed with, as these are necessary to enable her to enlist the aid of persons of widest influence throughout the State, but these should be held secondary to *personal* qualifications of the lady herself – as she must possess intelligence & cultivation of mind, *liberal patriotism*; and judgment and wisdom to enable her to use her vote with discretion in the Grand Council – at the Annual Meetings. She must also be in easy circumstances – as there is no salary attached to the office and some expense would be incurred in attending the meeting." (106) Cunningham made her appointments based on her personal knowledge of the appointee's character or upon the word of someone she trusted.

In late 1858 real estate entrepreneur William Markoe lived in St. Paul. Markoe was a native of Pennsylvania, who had become an Episcopal priest, only to notoriously convert to Roman Catholicism. Since Cunningham did not know anyone personally in Minnesota, she relied on the advice of Markoe's friend Capt. Percival Drayton of the U.S. Navy. Cunningham's secretary Christie Johnson contacted Markoe through

Drayton, asking "that you will have the kindness to suggest the names of such ladies in Minnesota, as you know would be suitable to fill – and would be likely to accept the Office." Markoe probably knew Sarah Sibley socially, and perhaps also through his land dealings with Gov. Henry Sibley, another major land owner in St. Paul. Sarah Sibley seems to have been Markoe's first, and perhaps only choice, as Christie Johnson crowed to New York Vice Regent Mary Morris Hamilton, "Mrs. Henry H. Sibley, wife of the governor of the State is admirably qualified for the office." (107)

In 1858 Sarah Sibley was the 35 year-old mother of four living children, Gussie, Sally, Franklin and Mamie. Her social position, education, and family connections qualified her to be vice regent. From the start of her marriage, she was an acknowledged leader in the early society around Mendota. Her friends and acquaintances beyond her immediate female relatives included the wives of Minnesota's most prominent men. Her ancestral family also provided impressive, patriotic credentials from important roles played in the Revolution. Sarah's sisters offered important local connections in business, politics and society. Additionally, Sarah's education made her articulate, intelligent, well organized, and confident. She showed how well she learned from childhood to be generous, pleasant, and virtuous – all necessary tools for successful fundraising.

Women gained access gradually to areas such as political, legal, social-geographical, and cultural activities in the mid-nineteenth century. Such women who pushed the boundaries of what was viewed as acceptable in the name of desired equality called themselves "strong minded" women. They boldly appeared in public and gave speeches on subjects they found important. The degree to which this was acceptable was a matter of protracted debate. Sarah's leadership in historic preservation was a product of the times in which she lived. Sarah Sibley boldly wrote public appeals, and certainly would appear in public on behalf of the effort, though it is not known whether she ever addressed those gatherings. And she would suffer from unkind public responses from newspapers as part of the debate on women's roles in public. (108)

Sarah accepted her new role with typical nineteenth-century "disinterest," as it was immodest to seek public offices even though she probably desired it. She wrote to Cunningham, "Among the ladies of St. Paul you could have found many more-efficient co-workers with you than myself, but I feel too deep an interest in the great and particular enterprise ... your association [is devoted], to decline to do what I can to promote its success." She optimistically added, "Every Minnesotian will be prompt to respond, to the extent of his or her ability, to a call for pecuniary aid." (109)

Thus began historic preservation in Minnesota. Presciently, she hinted at one circumstance that would determine success. Sarah lived in Mendota, a backwater settlement eclipsed by newcomers like Saint Paul six miles down and across the Mississippi. As vice-regent, Sarah would have to not only overcome distance from donors, but a number of other obstacles as well. Her foremost enemy was the lingering economic depression resulting from the Panic of 1857, when the land market crashed, banks closed, and hard money became very scarce. Competition from local charities worried her. As with other northerners, Minnesotans generally opposed slavery, therefore if they supported a charitable cause, they likely would not support saving a slave plantation. Most citizens could not distinguish between the worthiness to preserve a historic place and venerating what that place might stand for. Republican political opposition to her on account of her Democratic Governor-husband strengthened and grew throughout her campaign. The state's growing population was increasingly Republican. (110)

Even though she knew managing things from Mendota would be difficult, Sarah commanded a lot of cooperation, as seen in her statewide advisory board. Her husband's former enemy within the Democratic Party, Daniel A. Robertson, served in Ramsey County alongside future Republican Governor John B. Sanborn. Some of Sibley's business contacts, such as Orange Curtis, Richard Chute, Alexis Bailly, and Martin McLeod, also served on the board. (110)

Despite the lingering economic depression, optimism pervaded the streets of St. Paul. On September 3, 1858, St. Paul turned out for a grand celebration of the laying of the trans-Atlantic telegraph cable. Governor and Mrs. Sibley followed in a carriage behind the "Car of States" featuring young women from town representing each of the 33 states in the Union. Helen Sibley, Henry's Dakota daughter, represented Delaware, the first state in the Union. Despite the joy of the day, Sarah must have had some opinion of her husband's very showy display of his Dakota daughter. Those thoughts are lost to history. (111)

During the initial months of her historic preservation campaign, Sarah appointed lady managers around the state to assist her. By April 1859 the number would swell to 75 women, more women than customary "since our counties are large and sparsely populated," she wrote Cunningham. Disappointingly, few women responded to the call. Mary Bronson LeDuc, Frances Hubbell Berry, and Anne Loomis North all received invitations from Sarah to serve. Sarah told her friend Mrs. LeDuc that in Hastings "I wish you to bear the honors *gracefully* and *becomingly* (that is send me as much money as you can rake and scrape)." Mary's husband William Gates LeDuc observed to Sibley later that spring, "Mrs. LeD. is just now Exercised upon the Mt. Vernon quest," taking in $20 dollars that month. (112)

Frances Berry of Winona, wife of Minnesota's first attorney general, also declined her appointment, but nevertheless supported the cause with a donation of $5. Ann North also declined Sarah's appointment, writing to Anne Lewis that she "must conscientiously and respectfully decline ... I can give no aid to such an object without the assurance that it should no longer be a slave plantation." North may well have declined the invitation for another reason beyond abolitionist sentiments. Her husband John W. North was the secretary of the Minneapolis & Cedar Valley Railroad. He was frustrated with Governor Sibley's slowness in handling the Five Million Loan – an amendment to the state constitution designed to stimulate railroad growth and the state's depressed economy. John North blamed the governor for all of his railroad's disappointments. (113)

With everything in place, Sarah released an appeal to the people of Minnesota saying that although eastern women started the project, there was a place for Minnesota. Acknowledging the dire economic climate, Sarah assured everyone "the smallest offering will be thankfully received." (114)

The kick-off to the public campaign began with the celebration of Washington's birth. Sarah coordinated the day's festivities with the Saint Paul Mercantile Library Association, which sponsored lectures regularly. Although originally scheduled for the evening of February 22, the time was hastily moved up to 3 in the afternoon to share the day with the Pioneer Guard militia company. The Guard had received their new federal pattern uniforms one week before and was eager to show them off at a planned ball that same evening. Moving the patriotic exercise for the benefit of Mount Vernon to the middle of the day gave them one further event at which they might parade.

At 10 o'clock that Tuesday morning about forty men commanded by Captain Horace H. Western assembled at the armory. They formed ranks and marched to the Capitol. Recently returned from promoting Minnesota's railroad bonds in New York, Gov. Sibley, as commander-in-chief, and his staff were also decked out in their new uniforms. They reviewed the corps as it made several "evolutions" (changes in formation) on the Capitol lawn. After a respite at retired newspaper editor Daniel Robertson's house, they continued their march to Rev. John Mattock's First Presbyterian Church on Saint Peter and Saint Anthony streets.

The church was patriotically festooned: flags and evergreen boughs lined the chancel, and above the pulpit was a large portrait of George Washington. The inscription "Mount Vernon" below and "Washington" above encircled the picture in boughs. As a courtesy to her office, the Library Association provided complimentary tickets to Sarah and her husband. Promptly at 3 o'clock a national patriotic air played, and then Rev. Edward Duffield Neill arose to speak the invocation and prayer to more than 150 people in attendance. President John B. Sanborn of the Library Association read Washington's Farewell Address to the Continental Army.

Then came the main event: James Wickes Taylor, secretary of the Minnesota & Pacific Rail Road Company, delivered an oration in a "well known forcible and vigorous style." His original speech was to be on the life and character of Washington, similar to one that former Massachusetts Governor Edward Everett was giving throughout the North. Instead, Taylor devoted his time to the consideration of "Washington as the Representative Man of the West." He described Washington's life west of the Appalachians from 1748 to 1759 that shaped his character. Coincidentally, Minnesota's territorial period lasted from the Stillwater Convention of 1848 through statehood in 1858, which Taylor characterized as a centenary celebration of Washington's coming of age. Just as those years were significant in shaping Washington's life, Minnesota Territory set in place the institutions of the State. Turning his attention to the Mount Vernon Ladies Association, he remarked that 1859 was also the centenary of George and Martha's wedding, and that the Ladies' work would honor the Washingtons for many generations. He concluded by pointing to Washington's integrity as the glue that binds the fragile union together. Geographically, the many sections, he said, have little to do with one another except by Washington's influence.

The Philharmonic Society led the assembly in closing the program with an ode, written by local poet Dewitt C. Cooley, set to the melody of the "Star Spangled Banner." The Library Association realized $70 from 50-cent tickets for the Mount Vernon Fund. The organization entrusted the sum to Sarah to remit to Edward Everett. Sarah sent the donation to him on the first anniversary of Minnesota's statehood with many "obliging expressions." The Library, like many in the North, did not want to be perceived as supporting a slave plantation in Old Virginia, therefore effectively 'laundering' this donation and assuaging their consciences. (115)

Stillwater hosted the single most successful event for the MVLA on May 5. Henrietta Holcombe, whom Sarah had met at the railroad banquet in March 1857, guided the Lady Managers there. Together they organized an evening of entertainment at the newly opened Sawyer & Buck's Hotel on the corner of Second and Myrtle streets. The spacious hall was fitted for dancing; another room was set aside for chess and draughts (checkers); and still a third was reserved for conversation. Tickets were $2 each. The *Stillwater Messenger* reported "the tables, the decorations, and everything connected with the entertainment were arranged and conducted with exquisite taste." From this single event the women gathered $100, which Sarah again sent to Edward Everett. (116)

Following up the goodwill and patriotic feelings generated by the campaign proved difficult to do. The campaign appeared on the pages of a number of newspapers statewide, but did not garner universal acclaim. Republican papers opposed to Sarah's Democrat governor-husband, like the *Stillwater Messenger*, reported in March that Mount Vernon's current owner, John Washington, was hiring out his slaves. "We should think," wrote Andrew J. Van Vorhes, the paper's editor and husband of lady manager Elizabeth W. Van Vorhes, "Mr. Washington has been paid enough by the ladies of the United States ... to be able to do without hiring out his negroes." This sad note underscored general apprehension for directly aiding slavery.

The *Saint Anthony Falls Evening News* replied snidely to Mrs. Sibley's appeal assuring her "the people of St. Anthony are patriotic—very—and they will prove it by a generous subscription, if she will take their contributions in *lumber*; the association might want to build Mr. John Washington a coffin." Columbus Stebbins of the *Hastings Independent* wrote in his editorial of February 24, "Far and wide the Mount Vernon Association is extending its operations ... for the purpose of giving notoriety and character to every species of humbuggry and humbuggeries." Stebbins worried about the country being subjected to tacky tourist items like Mount Vernon hats, combs, and toothpicks. "The tomb of Washington needs no ornament," he opined. "The memory of Washington is embalmed in the heart of the nation, a more befitting monument than towering piles." As to the work of these women, "Let us stop it," Stebbins urged. He believed Americans could venerate Washington without a shrine.

Stebbins later reported John Washington contracted with a manufacturer to produce canes from Mount Vernon's wood. The *Saint Peter Minnesota Statesman* reported with disgust that Washington hired a 'daguerrean artist' to photograph tourists in front of the tomb.

The *Winona Republican*, perhaps influenced by Frances Berry, embraced Sarah's appeal calling it a "praiseworthy object" and urged those who had the ability to assist the fundraising campaign. The *Faribault Central Republican* did not comment on the project, merely printing a general Mount Vernon appeal. A number of Democratic papers like the *Hastings Weekly Ledger* and *Henderson Democrat* were entirely silent on the matter, which did not further the goals of the project. (117)

Although the campaign was intended to benefit Mount Vernon, some citizens took the opportunity to use the event for their own benefit. Saint Paul Post Office clerk George L. Lumsden used the fundraising campaign to perhaps change public opinion of him. Jailed under suspicion of stealing land warrants from the mails, the federal court in Preston convicted him later that summer. Lumsden published a letter in the *Pioneer & Democrat* to give expression to his generous donation of one dollar and to call attention to his "innocence." (118)

In Mendota, Mariah McCollum, the 35 year-old wife of a local Irish merchant, set the example locally for a number of resident former fur trade employees by giving $2. The McCollums were typical of the changing population of Mendota. A great number of Irish farmers moved into Mendota Township to take advantage of farmland well suited to familiar root crops and an established Catholic church. They seem to have gotten along well with the older residents who were also Catholic but of mostly French and Dakota heritage. (119)

As Mendota was changing, so was the rest of Minnesota, so much that Henry Sibley declined to seek a second two-year term despite encouragement to do so. Speaking at the Minnesota Old Settler's Association that summer he said: "In ten years, from a small settlement [Minnesota] had risen to a position in population, enterprise, and wealth – not exactly wealth," he winked significantly to the crowd indicating the ravages of the Panic of 1857. "But in population and enterprise equal to many of the old States," Sibley quickly quipped. His remark drew laughter, but pointed to the reasons he could not seek reelection. The state was hampered by the Panic, the fighting over a $5 million dollar state bond to finance building railroads on which railroad companies could make profits, a civil disorder in Wright County for which he had called out the militia, and a growing population that increasingly supported the Republican Party. (120)

Ever since her marriage sixteen years before, Sarah wanted to move into the growing urban center of Saint Paul. In early 1859 she thought a move was imminent, writing to her friend Mary LeDuc, "I think Mr. S. is beginning to find it a little inconvenient getting up and down to St. Paul. He is quite in the notion of building this summer, that we may be down next winter." While he was governor, Sibley boarded at the Fuller

House in St. Paul. A move would enable Sarah to personally lead the MVLA organization in Minnesota. When it became clear the move could not be made because of the continuing financial crisis, Sarah regretfully wrote to Cunningham resigning her life appointment as vice regent in late July. "My residence is six miles distant from St. Paul on the opposite bank of the Mississippi," she lamented. However, feeling responsibility for the MVLA in her state, she offered to stay on until a replacement could be appointed. (121)

Sarah reminded Cunningham of the scarcity of money in Minnesota and that in better times more could be collected. German immigrant Benedict Schmid, typical of many settlers, in Chanhassen Township of Carver County wrote in his diary for April 3 "since January I'm without money, which never happened before, since I'm in U.S.A." Schmid had lived in both Minnesota and Ohio for at least two years. Many in Minnesota looked for relief at harvest time later that year, as Abby Mendenhall of Saint Anthony happily hoped "Crops of all kinds promises a good yield," despite an early hard frost on September first. (122)

On November 3, 1859, Governor Sibley himself gave away his daughter Helen as the bride of Dr. Sylvester Sawyer in a ceremony held in the home of Helen's foster parents, William and Martha Brown. The Browns worked at the Red Rock Mission, in modern Newport, Minnesota, before trying farming and other pursuits. They had cared for Helen and for Catharine Forbes, the Dakota daughter of Henry Sibley's clerk William Forbes. Helen belonged to the Jackson Street Methodist Church. How much she interacted with her father and her step-family is not known. Evidence suggests that Helen had some contact with her father and perhaps with Gussie Sibley. Helen and Sylvester Sawyer then moved first to Milwaukee and then to Racine County, Wisconsin. Helen welcomed a little girl of her own on September 4, 1860. However, Helen contracted scarlet fever during labor and died. Her little girl, named Helen Mary Sawyer, also died a few days later.

Dr. Sawyer tried to learn all he could about his wife's relatives. In a letter to Helen's foster parents, Dr. Sawyer hoped that Sarah Jane Sibley might finally "banish all harshness and ill-will" for Helen. Too little of Sarah's papers remain to adequately characterize her thoughts about her step-daughter. Rebecca Marshall Cathcart who had glowingly admired Sarah at the July 4, 1849, ball recalled another incident for William W. Folwell. Sarah Jane wanted a Miss Spencer to alter some garment for her, but Henry "would not tolerate the seamstress at his table." When Miss Spencer was told of Sarah's offer and Henry's position, she reportedly replied that "people who did not stickle at associating with Squaws ought not to be too nice." As with any other White person of the era, it would be inconceivable for non-Whites of any heritage to share her table. But Sarah's opinion of Dakota people is hard to discern from remaining records. She knew and probably associated with the Faribault women who had Mdewakanton Dakota ancestry. Sarah had accepted the gift of a bag gladly from Mrs. LaFramboise (also Dakota) in 1851, and supposedly a bird cage from another Dakota woman. Therefore, Sarah's ill feelings for Helen could be interpreted as confined to Helen only as her husband's daughter by another woman. (123)

Nothing happened on the Mount Vernon campaign for many months after Sarah tendered her resignation in 1859. No word from the national leadership came, no funds were collected in the state, and no reports were sent to Sarah from her lady managers. Perhaps the worry of shocking events like the John Brown raid on Harper's Ferry in October, and subsequent trial and execution in December, held everyone's attention.

Amid the lull in MVLA activity, Minnesota Attorney General Charles Berry of Winona wrote his wife Frances Eliza Hubbell Berry, whom he lovingly addressed as "Frank." Sarah had tendered Frank the position of lady manager for Winona. "As I told you in my last, I should do so, I went home with Gov. Sibley Saturday evening. I had one of the best visits I ever had there. They are certainly a very lovely family." Drawing a delicate line between Frank's care of him and his experiences in Mendota, Berry would "not say her (Mrs. Sibley's) table is better than yours no others would be under the same circumstances but I could not suggest an improvement. The coffee was delicious."

Berry could relax because "Neither was there any 'gush' about the house, the table, or the dress of any one. In the evening we chatted in the library, till about 9 o'clock, when two of the Govs friends, with whom I was acquainted came in, where we played whist. The ladies retired. We had our cigars, & about ten o'clock refreshments were served by Mrs. S. & her sister Mary. After the gentlemen left, the ladies, except *Mrs.* Steele, came back & "visited" till about 12 o'clock."

Sarah Sibley thought of everything. "My room had been warmed" by running warming pans over his sheets. "All was neat & orderly as the most scrupulous care could make it. I slept sound." Sarah's domestic help ensured her instructions were followed, for "In the morning another fire was made in my room before I got up, my boots duly polished, & at breakfast another circle of smiling faces."

During Sunday's midmorning, "I read whatever I chose of the hundreds of books at hand. The library is a good one." When the family went to church, Berry accompanied them, observing "Mr. S. sometimes with us, & sometimes looking out for & attending to the children. The service was Episcopal," noted Berry who normally attended a Presbyterian church. "It is the only church in Mendota except the Catholic. It is built & owned by the Governor. The preacher is the old chaplain of the fort," Rev. Ezekiel G. Gear, "who had preached there some twenty years. But few attend."

Sarah's Sunday dinner was "splendid." Berry ate "Roast Turkey & other meats, sauces, all else to water" the mouth. "After the main course, came the cakes, coffee, & conversation. It was kept up a reasonable time, where we again went to the library & sitting room, they are the same, & talked till bed time." Sarah's mother Mary Steele "is a gem of a soul, just as good as you can wish."

On Monday morning Berry "bade them good bye & came to town.

Mrs. Sibley & her sister were very particular in making inquiries for you." He carefully reported that Sarah "had got your letter declining her appointment, – Money safe, & supposed she had answered." Berry had asked Sibley to ask Sarah about the donation as no receipt had come for the $5 sent. "It is however certain at last."

Then with a note for his daughter Kate, he wrote that "Mary Sibley had a great many questions to ask about her. Mary is a good little girl about three years old has large black eyes, & wears curls on her forehead and all round. She said she wanted me to tell her some stories. I told her all about Little Kate and the stories Little Katie tells. She wanted to learn them too. When I come home I will tell Katie more about Little Mary." (124)

Berry's visit ahead of the holidays probably lifted the gloom of separation from cosmopolitan St. Paul, at least momentarily.

Then just after the New Year, Sarah was surprised to receive a letter from Cunningham declining Sarah's resignation. Bewildered, Sarah stated more forcefully the reasons she should be relieved: financial embarrassments, her inability to affect things from Mendota, and her chronic illness going back to at least 1859. She added another reason, "the objects of charity among us are so numerous, ... and thus prevent those manifestations of good will to the Mt. Vernon Association." Other local charities successfully competed for what few discretionary dollars were left. Sarah believed she did everything in her power to help the Association, but it was "a sense of real mortification" to her that Minnesota had only collected $362 when neighbors like Iowa and Wisconsin each collected four times that amount. She rationalized that not much could be collected since "there never has been much wealth in this new and thinly settled State." And then alluding to her own family, she admitted "the recent financial disasters have operated ruinously even on those who had good reason to believe, that they were beyond the reach of such calamities." The Association would have to accept her resignation. (125)

The national crisis that Ann Pamela Cunningham hoped to salve with her patriotic effort to preserve and restore Mount Vernon was worsening. Extremists on both sides frightened moderates on the slavery question. Tensions ran high as political parties convened that summer to write platforms and select candidates for president.

In Minnesota, the Democratic Party worked to choose its delegates. Sarah's brother Franklin Steele did not often seek political office, but stood as a candidate to attend the Democratic National Convention in Charleston. He had been a leading candidate for Senate when Minnesota entered the Union. Henry Rice had been the first choice, but a block of voters in the legislature enabled former Illinois senator James Shields to pass Steele. Absolutely disappointed, Frank's wife suspected Henry Sibley of not supporting him fully. Henry Rice wrote an assuring letter to Annie both saying Sibley was for Frank's election but suggesting that Frank's naïveté cost him. Now on January 13, 1860, Frank again lost by not considering the situation. Governor Sibley arrived at the meeting just before the vote and declared his need to attend the Convention. He supported Stephen Douglas. A small group of "National Democrats" like Frank Steele supported John C. Breckinridge for president. The meeting elected Sibley in place of Steele, which set off Steele's longtime business associate John H. Stevens in a tirade. Stevens saw Frank's seat among Minnesota's delegates as a small honor due him, and failed to see the larger issue of the national debate on slavery. This vote permanently divided Steele from Sibley to the benefit of Rice, but also to the detriment of the Democratic Party. (126)

Former-Governor Sibley and Sarah traveled east together, she to visit family in Lancaster, Pennsylvania, while he continued on to Washington. Cunningham's new secretary, New Yorker Sarah C. Tracy, sent a note to Henry Sibley at Jackson Place in Washington City requesting a visit with Sarah. The national leadership wanted to get a handle on affairs in Minnesota, and to stress the fact Sarah's appointment was permanent by terms of the Association's charter. Since the note arrived late, and Sibley was to be on the 6:30 train the next morning, he suggested they could all meet once the convention closed. (127)

The Charleston Convention further exasperated Democratic politicians and, therefore, the sectional crisis. The bitter convention adjourned without selecting a national candidate because many Deep South delegates actually walked out when they did not get their way. The subsequent Baltimore convention allowed northern Democrats to select Sen. Stephen A. Douglas as its nominee. Southerners committed to "ruin or rule" attempted to be readmitted. The credentials committee on which Sibley served barred them from attending because they had walked out of the Charleston meeting. Henry Sibley usually committed himself to finding a middle ground, and perhaps it was his influence that briefly allowed a compromise of seating part of the number of Deep South delegates.

Six Miles from St. Paul

Not satisfied, southern delegates selected vice president John C. Breckenridge in a rival convention. Since the political process took longer than expected, Sarah decided to return home. Whether she was able to meet with Cunningham is unknown. (128)

    A very frustrated Henry Sibley returned home from the Baltimore convention in company with George L. Becker, who had run for Governor in Sibley's place in 1860, but lost to Alexander Ramsey. At Galena, they added to their group Governor Ramsey and Fort Snelling physician Major Robert C. Wood. Early in the morning of Independence Day these prominent Minnesotans boarded the *Key City* bound for St. Paul. Sarah suffered a severe attack that same morning "of what was supposed to be neuralgia in the shoulder, neck & head, but this culminated into a very dangerous form of pleuro-pneumonia." With a high fever, Sarah could breathe with only haltingly short pants, each eliciting burning pain in her chest cavity. The shallow breaths did not allow enough air in her lungs to either fully supply her pulmonary system or to efficiently expel mucus. When she did cough, it was uncontrollable and the result likely contained much blood. The burning sensation in her chest intensified greatly. When she regained control, Sarah would be surpassingly tired and extremely sore. Utterly stricken and in severe agony as she was, the family only dimly hoped Sarah might recover.

    Sarah was chronically ill. The context of Sarah's illness includes both enduring public criticism, shifting societal beliefs that may have emotionally confused her, and exposure to her children's constant illnesses. All may have contributed to a weakened immune system so that when the viral infection reached her lungs by 1859, she was less able to resist. With continued emotional stress, each attack left her increasingly susceptible to prolonged illness of worsening severity.

Another cause for alarm was Sarah's pregnancy of seven months. Henry told his friend William LeDuc that he was in "constant anxiety" for his wife's health. The "nightly watchings & loss of sleep, have pulled me down considerably." On July 21 her fever broke, and Sarah began to improve with careful nursing from her husband who had not left her bedside. (129)

Charles Frederick Sibley arrived on September 11, and Freddie, as his parents called him, thankfully was healthy. With his birth the Sibleys had the largest number of their children alive at once (five), and they hoped that no further deaths would occur. (130)

The Ladies Association and its business continued in earnest. Still the women hoped to avert the horrors of a civil war that seemed so imminent. Answering for his wife, Henry wrote Cunningham "I have delayed a reply … because I have had a faint hope that the state of Mrs. Sibley's health would enable her to address you herself." Though Sarah had been confined to her bed for four months, she still desired the Association's success. Accordingly, Henry repeated Sarah's request to be replaced as state vice-regent since Sarah's "health forbids any reasonable expectation that she will be able to leave her room for months to come." He then restated the reasons success in Minnesota seemed so unlikely: the immaturity of the state, the "revulsion of 1857," and competing local charities. He doubted that the 1860 harvest would do much more than cover existing expenses this year. (131)

Chapter 8: Strangers in St. Paul

Sarah remained bedridden for at least four months. By New Year 1860 she showed signs of recovery, though Henry worried about her recurrent attacks. He confided his fear to family friend William LeDuc: "she will not last long, as she has them more frequently than heretofore." Looking ahead, Sibley continued, "I shall be much relieved if the spring season finds her no worse than she is at present." (132)

Sarah felt well enough on March 1, to host a small evening party in Mendota for twenty guests. With seeming improvement in his wife's health, Henry wanted to take a trip to see family and friends in Detroit. He had long admitted to a friend there, Dr. Pitcher, that "Long as I have resided away from Detroit, I look back to it as my old home, which it would give me pleasure to return to, but that is hardly within the range of possibilities, except so far as a brief occasional visit is concerned." Henry and Sarah planned another trip back to Detroit, his "old home." But, "should she not decide upon a trip to Detroit, I will take her down to see Mrs. LeD., when the weather becomes settled," Sibley told his friend William LeDuc. (133)

Friends concerned with Sarah's health mention her in their correspondence with her husband. Former newspaper editor Earle S. Goodrich, who had covered the deteriorated state of Mount Vernon in 1854, requested "if [they] can perpetrate a joke on" Sarah's sister Mary

Steele, "particularly wicked, do it, and charge it to the account of your friend." (134)

In April 1861, the fragile national unity perished with the start of the Civil War, and the work of the Mount Vernon Ladies Association was paralyzed. The Association was hopelessly divided by the war to the point that all communication with Sarah ceased. Sarah Jane Sibley's brother-in-law Richard W. Johnson recalled in 1887 that his thoughts as a cavalry captain in April 1861 were far "from realizing the extent of the terrible struggle upon which we were about to enter." Sarah and Richard and their contemporaries were like any other generation in that regard, not knowing the full significance of events they experienced, nor how much the experience might change them. That distance from realization allowed life in Minnesota to retain some appearance of normalcy, such as a visit from Henry's sister Sarah A. Sibley, which lasted most of the summer. (135)

In March 1855, Richard Johnson made the leap from a second lieutenant of infantry to first lieutenant of cavalry after Congress created the new Second Regiment of Dragoons. Future Confederate generals Col. Joseph E. Johnston and Lt. Col. Robert E. Lee commanded the regiment, and Johnson had advanced to captain by December 1856. Johnson recalled in his memoirs that he and Lee debated the "what-ifs" of secession in regards to the army, apparently while at Jefferson Barracks in St. Louis, 1855-1856. Lee went with his native state of Virginia into the Confederacy, while conscious-bound Johnson felt he must remain loyal to his oath when the Civil War began.

Brigadier General David E. Twiggs of Georgia, an aged veteran of the War of 1812 and Mexican-American War, commanded the Department of Texas, where the Second was stationed in various posts. At the outbreak of the Civil War, in an act of treason, Twiggs first surrendered all federal soldiers, including Johnson, to Texas state authorities before resigning his United States Army commission to enter Confederate service. The terms of surrender stipulated that federal soldiers would go to Indianola, approximately 80 miles northeast of Corpus Christi, and await transportation back to the United States.

The steamer *Empire City* departed Indianola just before sunset with portions of the Second Dragoons and Third Infantry. As the steamer headed for Cuba, officers and their wives speculated about secession and how long it might be before they would return to their posts. While in Havana, *Empire City*'s passengers learned of the bombardment of Fort Sumpter in Charleston's harbor. With all due speed, the steamer made its way to New York City where the officers parted company, as Johnson recalled some fellow officers were "under the mistaken notion that their allegiance was due first to the States which gave them birth." (136)

Rachel and Richard proceeded from New York through Harrisburg, Pennsylvania, to visit remaining family before a brief visit to Louisville. From April through September of 1861 he served on the Upper Potomac River, and fought well at the Battle of Falling Waters. Johnson may not have placed loyalty to his native state of Kentucky first, but he was loyal to advancement. When Kentucky offered him a commission as Lieutenant Colonel, he, too, applied for leave to take advantage of the opportunity. In the fast build-up of the army, Richard subsequently accepted appointment as a brigadier general of volunteer soldiers (as opposed to the Regular Army) while he, Rachel and their three sons were still in Harrisburg, Pennsylvania. (137)

When the Civil War broke out in the United States, Sarah Jane Sibley had just passed her 38th birthday in February and looked forward to celebrating her 18th wedding anniversary in May. Sarah's vigorous frame and her bright and mirthful eyes all showed the rigors of continued childbirth and recurrent attacks from pleurisy. Her dark hair was thinning around the center part in her hair. Her husband retired from being governor the year before, and while she was still the vice-regent of the Mount Vernon Ladies Association in Minnesota, she, too, wished to be retired from that public life to catch her breath and recuperate.

Despite the nation at war and her precarious health, Sarah accompanied Henry on a "flying trip" to Detroit, as he wrote to his former Attorney General, Charles Berry of Winona. Sarah "is improving slowly, and desires her kind remembrances to Mrs. B." The Sibleys would like to have stopped in Winona for a visit on their return, "but as the babies were left at home, Mrs. S. could not be persuaded to tarry at any point on her way." Apparently the Berrys and Sibleys maintained a warm friendship for many years, strengthened by Charles Berry's weekend stay in Mendota 18 months before. (138)

"If I was not one of your forgiving, easy kind of persons," Sarah wrote to her sister Rachel Johnson in November, "I would not write the scrape of a pen to you, until you answered the last letter I wrote while you were in Texas." The Johnsons, after a disconcerting journey from Texas, had settled into Louisville, Kentucky, with their three sons: Alfred Bainbridge Johnson, 8, Richard Woodhouse Johnson, 6, and Henry Sibley Johnson, called Harry, 2.

"I was sick so long — and so long getting well, (and not right well yet) that I have become cross, selfish and lazy," Sarah lamented with frustration over undesirable character flaws brought out by her struggle with pleurisy. "I dont know when Mary wrote you last, but Mr. Sibley wrote to Genl Johnson some time ago, and I suppose it makes little difference what member of the family you hear from, so you hear." One character trait remained consistent: Sarah maintained correspondence with her family members, even if they responded slowly.

"Today is Sunday, and, oh! how lonely and dreary it is" in Mendota, Sarah complained. The first snow of the season flew as she wrote, "We have had most charming weather until now, so winter comes rather sudden upon us, but as Mr. S. says we have plenty to eat and wear, what more do we want." Sibley cheerfully kept Sarah's spirits up during her ailment.

Still desiring to make use of the culture she enjoyed, she complained, "Mendota is so dull compared to Louisville, dont you think so?" Even worse, "Our house is more lonely and quiet this winter than usual, Gussie has gone to Detroit, to spend the winter with her aunt Sarah Sibley, who was with us the greater part of the summer." Much as Sarah had done at the same age, Gussie would "pursue some of her studies, but not go to school." Then somewhat perplexed, Sarah commented Gussie "has rather a fine voice, and is a little ambitious to become a fine singer. I dont know how that will be, it does not seem in the family to be musical; well we cant tell what your voice or mine would have been, had they been brought out."

Sending her to Detroit "with her Aunt this winter" kept Gussie from "the young society [of teenage girls] in St. Paul" that Sarah did not think appropriate. "Their heads are filled with beaux and parties to be sure, there are a few exceptions." Like her mother, Gussie too wished to live in St. Paul, as she told her friend Carrie Gullagher in a rare note from February 1856.

Their sister-in-law "Anne is in her cottage home, as she calls it," on Robert Street in St. Paul. The Steeles built this home in 1851 on the southwest corner of what would become 6th and Robert Streets. For most of the time other family used it, as the Steeles still lived either in their old home south of Fort Snelling or in Georgetown in the District of Columbia. Abby and Tom Potts resided in Frank and Annie's St. Paul home until 1865, and the Johnsons also stayed there whenever they visited St. Paul. St. Paul's expanding commercial district consumed the house about 1888.

Annie lived "with her three grown up daughters, you may say, for Kate & Rosa are as tall as you or I." Mary, the oldest, "is a queer one still, [and] a hot secessionist when she can get anyone to hear her, which is very seldom." Sarah's niece Mary supported State Rights, an idea that states could veto Congressional action or even secede from the United States. Still having these daughters at home was helpful with the arrival of another child.

Frank and Annie's 10th child was a son, but Sarah commented that they "dont know whether to call it Charles or Bill." The Steeles chose William, after Frank's brother. Annie wrote after the birth of "Willie," that "I am done."

Sarah had gotten a letter from their childhood friend Abb Frazer "a few days ago. She said she was so sorry that she did not get to see you while in Harrisburg, some of her children were sick — and she had to hurry home. She wrote to you but received no answer, then wrote to somebody else to know where you were, and got no answer, altogether a very lame excuse, I thought for not being a little more civil." Abb was a single mother now that her husband Reah had died after his struggle with mental illness.

"The Third Regiment" of Minnesota Volunteer Infantry "left this the other day for Louisville or some place near it, I presume you might recognize a good many faces among them, they were a fine set of men, but miserable officers. It was a good pity that Gov. Ramsey secured such inefficient men. There are still six or eight hundred men in the Fort, which gives the place a lively appearance, poor fellows, it is rather a sad sight to see them go off, perhaps never to return," Sarah wrote with a romantic flourish. "When will this horrid war come to an end?" she asked with seeming impatience. American demand for swift and stunning results in any war, and done almost bloodlessly, is not new.

Sarah informed Rachel that "Mother's health is about as usual, is still troubled now and then with palpitation of the heart, altho she has not had a very bad attack lately, expects to go to St. Paul tomorrow to attend Quarterly meeting" of her Methodist church, possibly the Jackson Street church that her daughter Mary attended.

Sarah fretted "This will be a long dreary winter to us, for every one seems to wear a long face." Both the weather and the prospect of a continuing war worked on Sarah's fellow citizens. In cheerier news, Sarah wrote happily that "Your friends in St. Paul I believe are all well." Some had new children since Rachel last visited in the winter of 1859-1860. "*Your friend* Mrs. Ninninger I understand has been in St. Paul for the last time, her husband Johnny has taken to the white aprons and meat saw again, for which he is not to be despised." The Panic of 1857 ended the land speculation of the Ninningers in a proposed town northwest of Hastings, forcing John to resume work as a butcher. "I have not seen Mrs. Ramsey for a year, she lost a sister a short time ago."

Despite the war, emigration to St. Paul remained strong, as Sarah observed "quite a number of strangers in St. Paul this winter, have come for their health." St. Paul's climate was thought to be "salubrious" for any number of discomforts and ailments. Sarah closed hastily as her nurse had the day off to visit relatives, and Sarah needed to attend to her household.

(139)

For about the last two weeks of November the Sibleys experienced "very cold weather and good sleighing, but the mild and warm days for the last two weeks have caused most of the snow to disappear." In January, the Sibleys were likely among the 200 guests at Anna and Alexander Ramsey's party "given to members of the legislature & others." (140)

Throughout 1862 the war did not go well for the North, but there is no hint as to what Sarah may have thought. In June her thoughts about the Mount Vernon Ladies Association may have been stirred with the arrival of Edward Everett. She had sent him all of the money raised in Minnesota for the preservation and restoration of Washington's Virginia estate as Minnesotans did not want to directly send money to a slave plantation. Everett had "come to town at the instance of Young Mens Christian Association to deliver a lecture." Ever the good host, Governor Ramsey took Everett, the former governor of Massachusetts, "in a carriage to St. Anthony, Minnehaha, Fort Snelling, &c." Ramsey does not record whether the two were able to visit the Sibley house, and consequently, if Sarah ever met her "money-launderer." (141)

Alexander Ramsey returned to the Sibley House late on August 19, 1862. He hastily scratched in his diary, "Intelligence from Lower Sioux Agency" upstream from New Ulm on the Minnesota River in the south-central part of the state, "that Sioux had murdered several persons – also Iona, town Acton [in] Meeker Co. several more were killed." Ramsey went first to Fort Snelling to confirm the news, and then to Mendota to ask Sibley to take command of the volunteers at Fort Snelling. Ramsey needed Sibley to restore order in Southern Minnesota. Sibley extracted certain assurances before accepting command, such as no interference by army officers and complete control of the expedition. (142)

Women played vital roles in every aspect of the Civil War, and Sarah fulfilled the single most common one: a homefront wife. Just as Sarah had to adapt to being the Governor's Wife a few years before, with her husband's new position as a military officer, she had another new and equally informal position to fulfill. Unlike her husband's other public tasks where she could accompany him and bring their children, there was no place for dependents in the field. (143)

As a military wife Sarah had to endure Henry's extended absences from home in both 1862 and 1863, leaving her effectively as the head of the house. Managing the affairs of the house would add to her perceived responsibility for the health, life, and welfare of her children.

Entertaining her husband's superiors and subordinate officers demanded she learn additional military etiquette and protocol above and beyond the high standards she already maintained for social occasions. The rank order of officers and their wives added another layer of consideration in how to treat, seat, and serve people. Military order needed to be strictly observed, whether a guest was commissioned or merely married to an officer.

Six Miles from St. Paul

The campaign to restore order to Southern Minnesota effectively ended after six weeks. Ramsey had given Sibley the highest rank he could provide, that of Colonel. Congress promoted him to Brigadier General, which gave him broader powers.

"Gen. Sibley arrived home in Mendota on Sunday afternoon, and visited [St. Paul] yesterday," the *Pioneer* noted in its Tuesday November 18, 1862, edition. On his visit, Sibley accepted command of the Military District of Minnesota from his commanding officer, Major Gen. John Pope, who, with his family, departed five days later. Sibley later remembered Mendota during the Civil War, writing, "The volunteers from Fort Snelling ... used to resort in large numbers to Mendota, and occasioned so much tumult and disorder, that many of the families left that place." Sarah had already observed that he began "to find it a little inconvenient getting up and down to St. Paul" while he was governor in 1858-1859. Now he would have another regular public position in St. Paul until the Civil War might end, and since Sarah was "frightened nearly to death by the flying reports" of the Dakota War, the Sibleys also left Mendota during the war. (144)

Leaving their Mendota house must have held a mixture of triumphant and melancholy feelings for Sarah and her family. On the one hand, she could now be closer to friends and culture which very much defined her character. Yet she left behind the place that had defined her since her marriage. It was the place where seven of her children were born, and two of them were buried. She might have recalled the many parties she hosted and the many quiet evenings spent enjoying time with her family, as her sister Rachel vividly imagined in August 1852 from Texas. Looking in the parlor one last time, she might have thought of the marriages of two of her sisters. And, somewhat more melancholy, she might have visited the family burial plot near their home to recall her two dead sons. With the prospect of an end to her social isolation, Sarah looked forward to a new life in the big city and likely managed every detail of the move.

Despite the Sibley's importance to the entire state, their names were closely linked to Mendota. Although they were from Mendota and newcomers to the city, eventually Sarah was honored and well-thought of "as though a resident of this city, and indeed both the general and his wife are regarded almost as pioneer settlers in this city." Sarah could now engage in the social world of St. Paul as she had long desired, even if she bore the stigma of newcomer. (145)

Sarah and Henry moved their family to St. Paul about the first of December 1862. The 1863 city directory shows the Sibleys at 9th and Olive Streets, near St. Paul's Episcopal Church on the same corner. The neighborhood into which the Sibleys moved was the heart of St. Paul society. One historian remarked, "What made Lowertown a vibrant, comfortable place to live was its people and their network of social relationships." Gov. Ramsey mentioned in his diary that the Sibleys attended six of the same parties as the he did during their first three months in the neighborhood. One party on Sarah's 40th birthday featured more than 100 guests at the Sibleys' new residence on February 8,

1863. Sarah also hosted a major party in honor of her husband's commander John Pope, when he returned on a visit on May 28, 1863. (146)

Determining exactly where the Sibleys lived in Lowertown is difficult. Their neighborhood in Kittson's Addition is a grid that supported approximately 60 blocks of mostly middle class residential housing and commercial buildings near Seventh and Olive. St. Paul building permits which began in 1885 do not show any work for houses at the corners of 9th and Olive (Kittson's Block 12) and 12th and Olive (Kittson's Block 2), and therefore do not provide any details of the size of these two houses. The 1885 Sanborn Fire Insurance map shows the two likely houses. A house with a Mansard roof at 9th and Olive across the street from St. Paul's Episcopal Church certainly appears large enough to host a party of 100 as noted in Ramsey's diary. This house may have been remodeled from another style, and could certainly have stood on that lot in 1862-64. A slightly smaller frame house that stood where 12th would have intersected Olive remains as another possibility. (147)

The decennial census only hints at her neighbors while Sarah Jane Sibley lived on Olive. Historian Eileen McCormack suggests the commonality of Lowertown residents stemmed from "The majority of St. Paul's residents in these years had left their families thousands of miles away... [and] they had settled in an area where they were close to others and to their places of work and worship." The Sibleys were no different, except that they had lived in Minnesota prior to settlement, and therefore had a slightly different standing. The census certainly shows a mixture of

European ethnicity surrounding the Sibleys, but cannot suggest what, if any, relationships Sarah may have had with her neighbors. (148)

Chapter 9: This Community is Shocked

Life in Lowertown did not fulfill Sarah's hopes and dreams. Sarah Jane Sibley was three months pregnant in June 1863 while her husband was away on a punitive military expedition against Dakota warriors. When daughter Mamie died June 13, 1863, Henry Sibley lamented, "How dear to us this little child was, [God] alone knows & [Sarah] alone can tell how terrible is the blow I have received. God bless my poor wife and enable her to bear up under the fearful bereavement." Sarah held the funeral in the parlor of her Olive Street house, prior to interment in Oakland Cemetery. (149)

Less than a month later, Franklin Steele Sibley died just short of his tenth birthday. "This second bereavement since the departure of the General on the Indian campaign, has called forth, in a more than ordinary degree, the sorrow of the whole community," the *Pioneer* printed. Again, as was customary, Sarah held the funeral in the family home.

On January 11, 1864, Sarah gave birth to Alexander Hastings Sibley, named for her husband's brother. The 1864 city directory shows that the Sibleys resided at the corner of 12th and Olive that year. This may have been a mistake as maps of that era do not show the two streets intersecting. Proof is inconclusive as to precisely where the Sibleys resided in St. Paul between December 1, 1862, and July 1, 1864. Presumably with the amount of property they owned, the Sibleys resided in one of their properties. (150)

Six Miles from St. Paul

After Henry and Sarah Sibley moved to St. Paul, they searched for a permanent home for their large household. Developers Jacob and Martha Bass and the Sibleys moved in the same social circles, for instance attending a Whist party together at the Merrills' in August 1864. The Sibleys purchased the Bass' house for $25,000 and closed on the property on July 1 that year. (151)

Jacob and Martha Bass developed several suburban tracts for St. Paul, including 80 acres of land along Trout Brook just east of downtown. Border lands between bustling downtowns and agricultural fields of the country developed into suburban "country" housing in the Eastern United States beginning in the 1840s. Lowertown was one such border land, lying just outside of St. Paul proper. The original plat of St. Paul began with the river and ended on Seventh Street, and spanned from west to east from St. Peter Street to Wacouta Street.

St. Paul's residents were largely composed of Easterners from Ohio, Pennsylvania, and New York. Developers like the Basses from Vermont continued their occupation in their adopted state. Lithographs and drawings of St. Paul in the 1850s show early residential sprawl loosely based on picturesque enclaves like the 1857 Llewellyn Park outside of New York. St. Paul's enclaves were far less comprehensive than Eastern examples, often being only a few blocks in size owing both to competition for land and the effects of the Panic that limited developers' ability to buy larger tracts. The patchwork of additions to St. Paul by so many small developers contributed to these pockets, interspersed with row houses, shared parks and commercial blocks giving Lowertown a decidedly comfortable, if disorganized, feeling. Such disorganization contributed to the sense of place and nurtured the "network of social relationships." (152)

Unfortunately, Jacob and Martha Bass decided to build their suburban estate in 1857 the same year as the financial crisis swept across the nation. A common theory expressed in St. Paul was that frontier settlements were less susceptible to financial "embarrassments" than eastern cities. Yet hard money had all but disappeared from its streets within a month that fall, as Martha Bass remembered for her children, "The times grew harder that year and in '58 father could sell nothing, so found it impossible to finish the house." Land in St. Paul was at its lowest value in 1859, and would not begin to recover until 1861.

The Bass' house was a three-story Italian-style villa with "fine large doors and high ceilings" that on the inside were intended to impress visitors. On the outside, the narrow tall windows, low hipped roof crowning intricate details, and airy cupola gave onlookers the impression of a truly romantic building. The main part of the house was square with a rear two-story ell (wing) terminating in a one-story summer kitchen. The ell was nearly flush with the east side of the house and pointed toward Partridge Street, which paralleled Woodward Street to the north. The carriage house faced Partridge, conveniently not in the direction of the wind toward the dwelling. Also on the grounds stood an ice house, which was just east of a set of stairs running down from the dwelling to the carriage house. Along the west side of the ell ran a porch facing away from the carriage house and into a fine yard.

Jacob Bass employed 35 year-old builder T.S. McConnell, who brought all of the woodwork used in the house from Cincinnati, Ohio. After the shell of the house was complete, McConnell, his 28-year-old wife Mary, and infant daughter Virginia resided in the kitchen while work progressed. Because of a lack of hard money, Jacob and Martha wound up paying the workmen in residential lots in exchange for plastering and carpentry work to have their house ready to move into by August 1, 1858. (153)

Anna Ramsey, whose husband likewise had been at the Merrills' Whist party, called on her friend Sarah Sibley and found her "delightfully situated." However, the house "brings no happiness to her" as she had lost infant son, Alexander Hastings Sibley, one month after moving in. Little Alexander was just 8 months old. Adding to Sarah's cares was the illness of her mother, who followed her grandson in death on September 19, 1864. (154)

With the Civil War coming to an end, the Mount Vernon Ladies Association began reconstructing its efforts by notifying the vice-regents of the Grand Council of a meeting in late 1864. As Sarah was still technically a vice regent—having a life appointment—she received an invitation to attend. The Association likewise sent her invitations for 1865 and 1866. Having heard nothing, Miss McMakin, another of Cunningham's secretaries, wrote to William Markoe again to see whether "Mrs. Sibley has deceased or at least removed." Markoe gave the letter to John S. Prince, then mayor of St. Paul and Sibley family friend, forcing Henry to take action. He sternly affirmed to Markoe that all letters had been answered except the most recent invitation, that little or no communications were received since 1860, and that any direct correspondence would be promptly answered. (155)

When Alfred Brush Sibley was born on July 29, 1866, Sarah had been either pregnant or nursing for the better part of 22 years. There are several blank periods of time between the otherwise regular births of her nine children, suggesting the possibility of miscarriages. However, only one miscarriage is documented by her sister Abby in an undated letter. The effect of so many pregnancies on her health prompted brother-in-law Richard Johnson to ask Henry shortly after the birth of Alfred, "Don't you think it is high time to put a stop to these regular arrivals?"

According to one historian, large families were "accepted, if not prized," by early nineteenth-century American women. But birth rates throughout the century declined among native-born women. At the time of Sarah's birth in 1823, for example, the crude birth rate is estimated to have been 52.8 per thousand people. During Sarah's own pregnancies the number had fallen to 43.3, and by the end of the century it was 31.5. Rates among foreign-born women are thought to be about twice that of native-born. In 2006 the overall crude birth rate for the United States stood at 14.1.

Why Sarah had so many children may never be known, however, several possibilities are likely. First, as with foreign-born women entering the eastern United States, Sarah was also "foreign born" in the sense that she was not born in Minnesota, but rather in eastern Pennsylvania. Relocation to remote places statistically affects birth rates. One study suggests the increase in fertility is 23 to 33 percent higher in immigrant women than for women who remained in their native countries. Sarah may have been influenced by the sizes of households of her neighbors and peers. On average, Sarah's household is more than twice the size of her neighbors, and 20 to 30 percent larger than her peers. (156)

Other reasons for a large family could include: Sarah was a product of her own family, of which she was the last of nine children. A large family may have been seen as ordinary. Or, with the deaths of so many of her children, it is entirely possible that she sought to replace dead children to ensure a large family. There may have been some unspoken competition with her sisters Abby and Rachel, who had considerably fewer children, or her sister-in-law Annie Steele, who had 10 children. And lastly, Henry and Sarah may have opted not to use available methods of birth control.

Regardless of why Sarah had a large family, American expectations surrounding the size of family were changing. A woman's control of the size of family in that era depended on her situation. Just after Sarah's pregnancies in 1867, for example, New York had roughly 400 abortions performed. One Irish woman remarked of this practice, "We like large families of children, but American women kill theirs before they are born." Most such abortions were performed on middle and upper class women, among whom Sarah certainly could count herself. There is no evidence of Sarah's opinion of the practice, and with her many pregnancies there is little reason to believe she ever considered the procedure. Plus, such a notion ran contrary to her deeply held Christian beliefs. (159)

After one party on Thursday, November 14, 1867, a common household danger nearly cost the Sibleys their fine home. Their maid Maggie Murphy was making her evening rounds to tend the kerosene lamps. At the top of the stairs she tripped and dropped a lamp, which exploded. The burning kerosene splashed onto Maggie, setting her clothes afire. Her screams brought the family running. Maggie fell into 23-year-old Gussie Sibley's arms, badly burning them and her neck. Both Sarah and Henry suffered burns to their hands. Henry managed to roll Maggie in a carpet to extinguish the flames, but she was burned too badly and died a short time later. Gussie's uncles, Doctors John Steele and Thomas Potts, treated Gussie, Sarah, and Henry for their injuries. Henry informed his former business associate Hercules Dousman that while Sarah's and his wounds were nearly healed, Gussie "has undergone a lifetime of agony in the past six weeks." But "she suffers much pain while her wounds are being dressed but endures it with commendable resignation." (160)

Annie Steele returned to St. Paul from Georgetown, District of Columbia, in early September 1868. She visited the remains of her house near Fort Snelling, and the burial vault the Steeles once had near Minnehaha Falls containing the remains of four of her children. On September 10 she "walked round to Sarah's – find her rather low spirited," but "went out riding with Sarah to see Abby and to do some shopping" the next day, which she "found ... dull and uninteresting." Annie spent parts of eleven of the next 18 days with either Sarah or Sarah's daughter Gussie. On September 17 Annie dined at the Sibleys' along with Douglass Pope and Sarah's sisters Abby Potts and Mary Steele. (161)

Captain Douglass Pope was the nephew of Henry Sibley's commanding officer, Maj. Gen. John Pope. Douglass had come west with his uncle in 1863 and presumably met Gussie Sibley at any number of social events in St. Paul, prior to departing on the punitive expedition with his prospective father-in-law that summer. He served as Sibley's Inspector General on staff with several other captains, thus Sibley had a firsthand opportunity to observe the habits of his daughter's suitor. A poem about Douglass and the others on Sibley's staff had appeared in the St. Paul *Pioneer* in December 1864. The anonymous writer pictures Pope "with his heels upon the window," acclaiming him as a "woman slayer, fisher, hunter, steed-destroying pigeon hunter." Much of the poem was filled with sarcasm, so saying Pope was something of a womanizer might be tongue-in-cheek.

Pope and fellow staffers Captain Rollin C. Olin and Lieutenant Thomas Larke also spent hours playing baseball. Olin organized the Excelsior Club comprised of military officers. Sarah's brother-in-law Tom Potts, medical purveyor for Fort Snelling, served as scorekeeper. Sibley seemed partial to sporting, especially hunting and fishing, if not also baseball. In 1867 when Pope and Olin organized the Minnesota Base Ball Players Association, they named their former commanding officer its president. Perhaps Pope's penchant for whiling away hours smoking a pipe, lounging about with his feet on the window sill, or playing baseball suggested a certain amount of laziness, which contributed to Henry and Sarah's wish that their daughter might choose someone else. (162)

"Gussy and I went out walking," Annie recorded in her diary on September 25, and "spent evening … discussing Gussy Sibley's marriage." The next "evening Sibley and Sarah called," and "Sarah asked us all to come to Gussy's marriage at 8 o'clock Tuesday morning." (163)

Rising at 6 a.m. on September 29, Annie "dressed in my blue silk to go to Gussy Sibley's wedding. She was married at half past eight o'clock," as apparently all waited, hoping Sarah Sibley would recover from coughing enough to attend. However, "Sarah Sibley [was] too sick to see her married." Over the years this episode has been interpreted in conjunction with Henry and Sarah's objections to Capt. Pope as a passive way of expressing her disdain for the marriage. However, Henry told Bishop Henry Whipple, "a probation of five years has testified to their deep mutual attraction, and we could no longer with reason interpose." Additionally, Sarah's expectations for behavior demanded better of other people, and particularly from herself. With the change in season and intense house cleaning for the wedding that launched particulates into the air, Sarah's breathing inflamed the infection in her lungs, causing Annie to pronounce the event "a sad wedding." Three days later when Annie visited, Sarah was still very ill. Even two weeks after the wedding Sarah was still unable to leave her room. Sarah's chronic illness incapacitated her at inconvenient times, including Gussie's wedding. (164)

Six Miles from St. Paul

In the spring of 1869 Sarah answered her friend Mary LeDuc's invitation to come to Hastings for a visit, writing, "we have commenced to clean house ... If Gussie was only here, she might take charge of the house during my absence." Her husband was of no help in this endeavor as "he is really not able to devote one half day to me." Meanwhile, her two-and-a-half year old son Alfred "rules this house, or at least he would like to." (165)

With her oldest daughter married and living in Illinois, Sarah Sibley attended to spring cleaning without her principal lieutenant. Sarah looked forward to a visit "the last of May or the first of June" in Hastings with her friend Mary LeDuc. While Sarah and her contemporaries with respiratory ailments knew their lungs were affected seasonally, they attributed the phenomena to the change in seasons. Interior environments and particulates in the air were not well understood for the impact on human health.

The dust, soot, and fibers from the winter flew into the air and triggered yet another respiratory attack on May 14. With the chronic nature of the illness, no one took this attack for anything more than another in a long line of routine attacks. On May 18, Sarah's condition took a turn for the worse. Her husband immediately summoned their daughter Gussie by telegraph to return to St. Paul from her mother-in-law's house in Springfield, Illinois. Gussie Pope arrived at her parents' house on Woodward Street on the evening of May 20.

When the Sibleys relocated to St. Paul's Lowertown, they began attending St. Paul's Church, an Episcopalian congregation. In the 1920s the congregation removed from Lowertown to Summit Avenue and became known as St. Paul's on the Hill. Sarah thought quite highly of Pastor A.B. Patterson's preaching.

Patterson joined the gathered family because Sarah had called for him to administer the Sacrament of Holy Communion. Sarah knew the sacrament held the forgiveness of her sins through the Word of God, which she habitually read. Thus she desired the reassurance of her salvation prior to death. Knowing that her death was near, Sarah "called her family around her bed and spoke to them parting words of comfort and advice." Both of these activities were customary for the day. Partaking in Holy Communion was a statement of her faith, although sometimes mistaken by others as a final absolution for sin. And final words spoken by the dying were considered more honest and sacred since the dying person was much closer to eternal glory than those who would go on living. The family kept watch the entire night, and at approximately 9 the next morning May 21, 1869, Sarah died at age 46 years, 3 months, and 13 days.

"This community is shocked," announced the *Daily Dispatch* Friday afternoon, only a few hours after Sarah's death. "Her illness had been of such brief duration that comparatively few were aware of it until her death was announced." (166)

The funeral took place on Sunday afternoon at 2 o'clock. Unlike the funerals of her two children in 1863, Sarah's funeral was not held in the family home, but at St. Paul's Church at 9th and Olive streets. The church was "crowded to overflowing" with the "presence of a large number of friends." Some of the city's most prominent and influential men were pallbearers, taking the casket from the church to an awaiting hearse. The large cortege followed the horse-drawn hearse slowly up Olive to Grove, and then north toward Oakland Cemetery, which her husband had been instrumental in establishing. The graveside service commenced at the family plot just inside the west entrance to the cemetery. With prayers and scripture readings Patterson comforted the bereaved with the assurance of a blessed reunion in heaven. The pallbearers lowered the casket containing Sarah's body into the ground to rest near the remains her children, mother, and Aunt Betsy Humes. (167)

Sarah and Henry's longtime friend Alexander Ramsey borrowed a horse and buggy and drove down to see grief-stricken Henry for several hours at their home on the following Tuesday. Henry remained in the house until his death in 1891, and never forgot his wife whose presence was closely linked to the St. Paul home she longed to have while they lived most of their married life in Mendota. (168)

Epilogue: Remembering Sarah Jane Sibley

J. Fletcher Williams wrote in 1894 of Henry Sibley's "great sorrow, the death of his wife." Sarah's death ended "years of quiet domestic enjoyment" for Henry and his family. Through the remaining years of Sibley's life, until 1891, "he bore this loss patiently and resignedly, bearing with him ... the memory of the quarter century of married life that had been so happy and blest." (169)

Although Sibley and his children cherished Sarah's memory, she faded from public memory over time. She died at a young age, but had she lived longer she would have been present at the gatherings of Minnesota's pioneers to add to Henry's stories, and tell some of her own. As the nineteenth-century waned, the expansion of women's roles slowed, and the emphasis on public men increased, which relegated Sarah's work into Henry's shadow. As Minnesotans approached the state's jubilee in 1908, they further magnified his work as many alive then could at least recall Sibley in his old age only 17 years before. Finally, Sarah's memory was physically destroyed when the Minnesota Historical Society returned all of the personal papers of the Sibleys to their children.

Historic preservation work also faded. With Sarah's death the efforts of the Mount Vernon Ladies Association permanently ceased in Minnesota for the next twenty years until Rebecca Flandrau, one of Sarah's lady managers, accepted appointment as the second MVLA vice-regent for Minnesota. Perhaps the Minnesota Valley Historical Association renewed interest in preservation in the 1880s by marking many of the events associated with the U.S.-Dakota War of 1862. In 1910, forty years after Sarah's efforts, the Daughters of the American Revolution used the same patriotic, private, woman-led methods pioneered by Sarah Sibley a half-century earlier to rescue Sarah's stone house in Mendota, dubbing it the "Mount Vernon of Minnesota." (170)

Henry never remarried and the quality of his marriage faded from public memory. When his brother-in-law Tom Potts relocated to Duluth in 1871, Sarah's sister Abby Potts and her children came to live with Henry. Tom felt his prospects for earning a better living might improve in the booming Lake Superior port, but he could not climb the hills because of a weakened heart. After his death in 1874, speculation in St. Paul supposed marriage might be imminent for Henry Sibley and his sister-in-law who co-habitated his house on Woodward. Abby Potts served as Henry's hostess, and Henry supported her and provided a place for her two daughters to have a double wedding in his house. Henry and Abby traveled together as he sought relief from old age maladies. And, Henry provided for Abby in his will.

Memory is often tied to physical places, but finding the places Sarah Sibley knew can be challenging. The town of Steelesville in Pennsylvania all-but died when the railroad bypassed it. The 1850 census shows only 77 people living there. By 1870, historians Franklin Ellis and Samuel Evans state the mills that Sarah's brother Bill attempted to keep going were in ruins. Still, in 1893, there were 70 people living there despite the nearest railroad being 5 miles away in Altgen. (171)

Frank Steele's cottage south of Fort Snelling, in which Sarah Jane briefly lived, is also gone. Evolving military needs remodeled Fort Snelling in the 1860s, 1880s, 1910s, and 1930s, such that nothing probably would look much the same to Sarah. Even the rebuilt schoolhouse that doubled for a chapel where she married Henry Sibley probably would not look precisely the way she experienced that building.

Her first house still stands in Mendota, preserved by the Minnesota Society of the Daughters of the American Revolution for 85 years prior to the Minnesota Historical Society accepting the site into its historic sites network in 1996.

The two or three houses Sarah called home in Lowertown are gone. Finding out where those stood is difficult.

Lowertown suffered from its borderland status, proximity to St. Paul proper, and the natural grade of Trout Brook falling from the upland bluffs to St. Paul's lower landing. With the advent of rail transportation Lowertown was simply in between where the rails had to go and the markets of St. Paul's downtown. When the Great Northern ran a spur along 8th Street in the 1870s, the neighborhood began to decline. The house the Sibleys bought in 1864 for $25,000 sold for only $30,000 in 1892 as Henry's children liquidated the family's estate. By the mid-1950s the last of the residences disappeared and today the neighborhood is office space, commercial buildings, and trucking firms.

Six Miles from St. Paul

There is very little left of Olive Street, which still intersects with Grove, but intersections south of there in the neighborhood of Sarah's first Lowertown houses are gone. Woodward Street faired even worse. The only segment remaining is about a block long terminating at Payne Avenue just north of Seventh Street. Madison and Monroe streets leading to Woodward are also gone. The sites of Sarah and Henry Sibley's suburban houses in Lowertown do not exist. The stately house on Woodward stood about at the edge of the parking lot for the modern office building that houses the Minnesota Department of Natural Resources staff and the adjoining rail line.

The pavement of so many parking lots and lack of shade hardly suggest the boulevards lined with mature trees that attracted St. Paul's elite. The boxy utilitarian commercial buildings replaced the richly detailed houses, billboards replaced the spires of the many churches, and the busy energy of modern people replaced the comfortable and stately pace of life in a mid-nineteenth-century residential neighborhood. The Lafayette Freeway's northern terminus at East Seventh Street brings thousands of vehicles through Lowertown everyday. Lowertown is really no longer a borderland but a transitional transportation zone between downtown St. Paul and Dayton's Bluff. Rail lines have long severed Lowertown's historic connections to the river via the lower landing, and obliterated nearly the entire original pattern of Kittson's Addition. Lowertown's historical integrity from its earliest days, including those that illustrate Sarah Sibley's earnest desires to live in cosmopolitan St. Paul, is lost forever. (172)

Sarah's descendants still remember Sarah through genealogy and family stories. Sarah and Henry's four surviving children at the time of Henry's death were grown. Gussie was a widow with three grown children. Her sister Sallie had married Elbert A. Young, and had three children. Their brother Fred married Constance Locke, but they did not have any children. Alfred, who "ruled the house" at the time of Sarah's death, married Anna Thompson in 1892. While Alfred and Anna's daughter lived to adulthood and married, their son Henry Hastings Sibley died in childhood. There are no descendants that bear the surname Sibley.

"Future Minnesotans may like to know these intimate facts of her history," wrote Sarah's first historian, Julia Johnson. (173) How Sarah has been remembered over time has changed with the times since her death until present. How she will be remembered will continue to change as each succeeding generation applies the lessons of her life to theirs. The one constant is that she should be remembered.

"Mrs. Sibley was a warm hearted Christian lady, and possessed a host of friends who will sincerely mourn her sudden death and tenderly cherish her memory," the *Daily Dispatch* wrote when she died. Retired Civil War general Christopher C. Andrews remembered that she was a "lady of superior accomplishment and worth."

Others like J. Fletcher Williams in 1894, the first employee of the Minnesota Historical Society, wrote that Sarah Sibley was "admirably fitted to adorn the prominent station in society which she occupied for so many years in Washington and St. Paul." Charles E. Flandrau, whose wife

Rebecca assumed Sarah's post as vice regent of the Mount Vernon Ladies Association in Minnesota, "Mrs. Sibley was a lady of superior traits of character and general worth, a most befitting companion for her gallant and distinguished husband, and beloved by all who knew her." Yet all these historians wrote were accolades without detail. (174)

Even when the Daughters of the American Revolution (DAR) opened the Sibley House to the public on June 14, 1910, Sarah was said to be "the most romantic, the most distinguished pioneer of early Minnesota that she will be remembered, admired and loved best." The public memory of Sarah over the years has largely been the responsibility of the DAR. When a compendium of biographies of prominent Minnesota women was printed in 1924, the DAR made sure that Sarah Jane Sibley was included, even though she had been dead for 55 years – generations of Minnesotans had never met her. Although the bulk of the entry recounted her husband's life, the biography remembered her as "having great personal dignity, unlimited hospitality, and great tact." (175)

Succeeding generations have remembered Sarah Sibley in the context of their own times. With many of Minnesota's pioneers passing away, along with the generation that fought the Civil War, people turned to romantic notions of when the state was new. Indeed at the turn of the twentieth century a wave of patriotism surged along with romanticism to create very nationalistic feelings. The tender and glowing words of Andrews, Williams, and Flandrau, all members of Sarah's generation, fit this era well. Julia Johnson and the DAR's writing reflect their need to establish the significance of the story that the Sibley house could tell.

Although bound to Sarah by family relationship, the goal was to persuade people to visit the site and learn an example of virtue in the public deeds of her husband.

Each time Sarah's story is told, new interpretations will be added in order to make her relevant. In addition to emphasizing what is important to that generation, hopefully Sarah's complex character, and all very human condition, will come to the fore. Each person wants to be valued and remembered as they see themselves, with dignity, respect, and fairness. Sarah Sibley might want to be remembered as well educated, responsible for her family and extensive friends, a capable and effective manager, a competent leader in society and historic preservation, and a Christian who strove to lead a Christ-like life. In addition to these, she might want to be remembered as a daughter, sister, wife, mother, and lover. Sarah Sibley led a life worthy of remembrance.

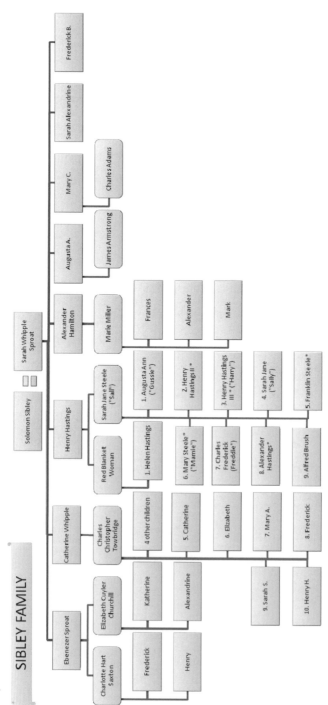

SIBLEY FAMILY

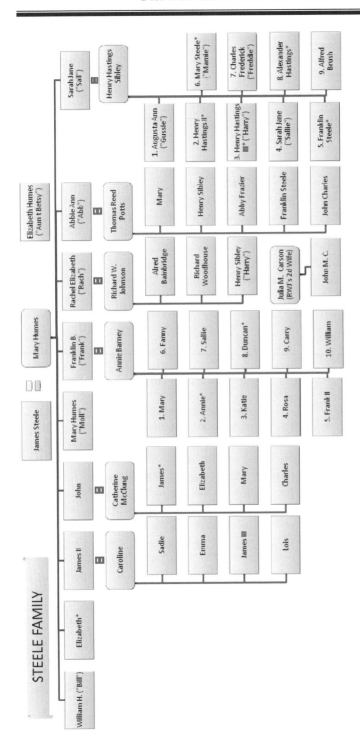

End Notes

DAR: Daughters of the American Revolution
HHS: Henry Hastings Sibley
MHS: Minnesota Historical Society
MVLA: Mount Vernon Ladies Association
SHA: Sibley House Association
SJS: Sarah Jane Sibley

(1) Rhoda R. Gilman, *Henry Hastings Sibley: Divided Heart* (St. Paul: MHS Press, 2004). The Steele family background originally appeared in: David M. Grabitske, "Sarah Jane: A Lady's Frontier in Minnesota," *Midwest Open Air Museums Magazine* 20/3 (1999): 20-32.
(2) SJS to HHS, March 20, 1856, and set of poems, Sibley House Association Collection. Julia M. Johnson, "Mrs. Sarah Jane Sibley," in Robert S. McCourt, *The History of the Old Sibley House*, Official DAR Souvenir, 1910 (quote). HHS to Henry F. McCloskey, June 6, 1853, Sibley Papers.
(3) SJS to Rachel Elizabeth Steele Johnson, November 18, 1861, Sibley Papers.
(4) SJS to William G. LeDuc, May 20, 1858, William G. LeDuc Papers, MHS.
(5) Franklin B. Steele to HHS, April 6, 1842, Sibley Papers.
(6) Steele to HHS, April 9, 1842, Sibley Papers.
(7) Katherine W. Vaughan, *General Henry Hastings Sibley* (St. Paul: Katherine W. Vaughan, n.d.): 9. Nathaniel West, *Ancestry, Life and Times of the Honorable Henry Hastings Sibley, LLD.* (St. Paul: Pioneer Press Publishing Co., 1889): 80-86. Hercules Dousman to HHS, March 22, 1843, Sibley Papers.
(8) George Woytanowitz, "Chronicle of the Sibley Historic Site," (unpublished manuscript): 1842.
(9) Julia M. Johnson, 26. Elizabeth Donaghy Garrett, *At Home: The American Family, 1750-1870* (New York: Harry N. Abrams, Inc., 1990): 217-248.
(10) Woytanowitz, "Chronicle," 1847; David M. Grabitske, "Minnesota at the Entry" (SHA unpublished manuscript): 11-12; Lisa A. Krahn, "Was Jean-Baptiste a Spy?" *Mudduck: Newsletter of the Upper Mississippi Brigade* (May 2000): 15.
(11) Bruce A. Kohn, "Wingings of the Bird: Governor Henry Sibley and his Daughter Helen from his Dakota Indian Family," unpublished manuscript dated February 6, 2008, in author's possession. Grabitske, "Entry," 5-7. Woytanowitz, 1841. Hercules Dousman to HHS, March 22, 1843, and Thomas S. Williamson to HHS, January 18, 1845, Sibley Papers. Another possible child is Henry Milor.
(12) First Presbyterian Church Papers, 1835-1871, MHS Collections. First Presbyterian started out as St. Peters Church, and was subsequently reorganized as Oak Grove Church, Minnehaha Falls Church, and then First

Presbyterian in Minneapolis.

(13) Observations on the Sibley House and its construction are the author's from personal experience. For the claim that soldiers worked on the Sibley House, see Lawrence Taliaferro to HHS, January 18, 1849, Sibley Papers: "as if *Soldiers* have not worked over & often for *yourself* & other citizens at the post & well as fir the Missionaries when placed on *pass* or furlough for few days – to go where they desired." Sibley genealogy: James Scarborough Sibley, *The Sibley Family in America, 1629-1972* (Honolulu, 1972): 151.

(14) Sibley, *Sibley Family*, 41. Elizabeth F. Ellet, *Pioneer Women of the West* (Philadelphia: Porter & Coates, 1850): 215-225.

(15) HHS to Frederick B. Sibley, February 20, 1844, Sibley Papers.

(16) Jane C. Nylander, *Our Own Snug Fireside: Images of the New England Home, 1760-1860* (New Haven and London: Yale University Press, 1993): 20-53. Ann Marcaccini and George Woytanowitz, "House Work: The DAR at the Sibley House," *Minnesota History* 55 (Spring 1997): 186-201. Barbara A. Levy and Susan Schreiber, "The View from the Kitchen," *History News: The Magazine of the American Association for State and Local History* 50/2 (March/April 1995): 16-20.

(17) Sibley Family Bible, "Births" and "Deaths." SHA Collections.

(18) Nancy Schrom Dye and Daniel Blake Smith, "Mother Love and Infant Death, 1750-1920" *The Journal of American History* 73/2 (September 1986): 329-353.

(19) Nylander, *Our Own Snug Fireside*, 26, 30. Abby Steele was on hand for Harry Sibley's birth in 1848, and sisters Mary and Rachel were frequent residents of the Sibley household beginning in the summer of 1848.

(20) William H. Forbes to HHS, December 8, 1846, Sibley Papers.

(21) Potts Family Bible, SHA Collections. Thomas R. Potts to HHS, September 14, 1848, Sibley Papers. Bill for Medical Expenses, July 23, 1847 to June 1, 1848, Sibley Papers.

(22) Nylander, *Our Own Snug Fireside*, 20-53. Elisabeth Donaghy Garrett, *At Home: The American Family, 1750-1870* (New York: Harry N. Abrams, Inc. Publishers, 1990): 217-248.

(23) Gilman, *Divided Heart*, 105-106.

(24) Thomas R. Potts to HHS, September 14, 1848, Sibley Papers.

(25) SJS to Abby Steele Potts, undated fall of 1848, Livingston Papers, Ramsey County Historical Society. Reminiscence, May 1892, 3, Ellen Rice Hollinshead Papers, MHS.

(26) Reminiscence, 4-6, Hollinshead Papers.

(27) Franklin B. Steele to HHS, November 21, 1848, Sibley Papers.

(28) Thomas R. Potts to HHS, January 24, 1849, Sibley Papers, MHS. Rachel E. Steele Johnson to SJS, April 29, 1857, Livingston Papers, Ramsey County

Historical Society. John Steele to Gilbert Cope, February 14, 1881, Gilbert Cope Papers, Lancaster County Historical Society. Tenth Decennial Census, Coulterville, (Randolph County) Illinois, June 15, 1880. *Combined history of Randolph, Monroe, and Perry counties, Illinois.* Philadelphia: J. L. McDonough & Company, 1883. E.J. Montague, *A directory, business mirror, and historical sketches of Randolph County.* Alton, IL: Courier Steam Book and Job Print House, 1859.

(29) Steele to HHS, December 18, 1848, Sibley Papers.

(30) Potts to HHS January 24, 1849, Sibley Papers.

(31) "Henry Mower Rice," *Minnesota Historical Society Collections* (1894): 656.

(32) St. Paul *Pioneer*, May 19, 1849.

(33) Theodore C. Blegen, *Minnesota: A History of the State*, 2d Edition. (St. Paul: University of Minnesota Press, 1975): 163. Helen McCann White, *Guide to the Microfilm Edition of The Alexander Ramsey Papers and Records* (St. Paul: Minnesota Historical Society Press, 1974): 6.

(34) HHS to Alexander Ramsey, May 24, 1849, Sibley Papers. Alexander Ramsey diary, May 27, 1849, Ramsey Papers, MHS. Minneapolis *Journal*, interview with Alexander Ramsey, May 11, 1901. HHS to Ebenezer Sproat Sibley, June 16, 1849 and to Charles Trowbridge, July 11, 1849, Sibley Papers.

(35) St. Paul Pioneer, July 5, 1849. Rebecca Marshall Cathcart, "A Sheaf of Remembrances," *Minnesota Historical Society Collections* (1900): 524. Grabitske, *Lady's Frontier*, 20. MHS Etiquette Item, Invitation to Grand Anniversary Ball, July 4, 1849.

(36) HHS to Dear Sir, August 29, 1849; to Henry L. Moss, August 11, 1849; and to Frederick B. Sibley, August 11, 1849, Sibley Papers.

(37) HHS to Edmund Ogden, August 29, 1849, Sibley Papers.

(38) Alexander Ramsey diary, September 8 and 21, October 12 and 18, and November 10, 1849; Nancy Goodman and Robert Goodman, *Paddlewheels on the Upper Mississippi, 1823-1849* (Stillwater, MN: Washington County Historical Society, 2003): 127, 134.

(39) HHS to Martin McLeod, December 16, 1849, Sibley Papers.

(40) HHS to John B. Blake, April 29, 1851; to Solomon D. Jacobs, June 16, 1851, Sibley Papers. Seventh Decennial Census (1850) 4th Ward, Washington City, D.C. HHS to John B. Blake, September 6, 1851, Sibley Papers.

(41) Thomas R. Potts to HHS, January 18, 1850, Sibley Papers.

(42) Franklin Steele to HHS, March 12, 1850, Sibley Papers; Richard W. Johnson, *A Soldier's Reminiscences in Peace and War* (Philadelphia: J. B. Lippincott & Co., 1886): 56-57. John H. Stevens to HHS, March 30, 1850; Captain Bvt. Major Samuel Woods to Major Don Carlos Buell, May 4, 1850; and, John H. Stevens to HHS, May 22, 1850, Sibley Papers.

(43) See DAR *The Romance of Mendota*, repr. 1995.

(44) Alexander Ramsey to HHS, March 18, 1850; Thomas R. Potts to HHS, May 29, 1850; HHS to Alexander Ramsey, June 26, 1850; and to William H. Forbes, July 11, 1850; Frederick B. Sibley to HHS, August 1, 1850, Sibley Papers.

(45) HHS to Alexander Ramsey, August 6 and August 15, 1850; Alexander Ramsey to HHS, August 29, 1850, Sibley Papers.

(46) HHS to Alexander Ramsey, July 19 and August 28, 1850, Sibley Papers. Gilman, *Divided Heart*, 115.

(47) Frederick B. Sibley to HHS, September 9, 1850, Sibley Papers.

(48) Alexander Ramsey diary, October 19, 1850, Ramsey Papers. HHS to Joseph LaFramboise Sr., October 25, 1850, Sibley Papers.

(49) The events of the Johnson wedding are difficult to assemble. According to the Johnson's marriage certificate signed in 1865, they were married at the Sibley House, and both Henry H. Sibley and Alexander Ramsey were witnesses. The St. Paul *Pioneer* likewise reports the marriage in the Sibley parlor, in its October 31, 1850 edition. However, Alexander Ramsey's diary indicates the Johnsons were married at Fort Snelling. Anna Jenks Ramsey had attended, and her husband Alex joined her later in the day. They spent the night at Franklin Steele's house. See Alexander Ramsey Papers diary, October 20, 1850.

(50) Whortley Journal, November 10, 1850, MHS. Frederick B. Sibley to HHS, November 24, 1850, Sibley Papers.

(51) Fred to HHS, December 16, 1850; Potts to HHS, January 7, 1851; Fred to HHS, January 7, 1851; and Potts to HHS, January 21, 1851, Sibley Papers.

(52) Fred to HHS, December 16, 1850, Sibley Papers. Francis B. Heitman, *Historical Register and Dictionary of the United States Army* (Washington: Government Printing Office, 1903; repr. University of Illinois Press, 1965; repr. Olde Soldiers Books, 1988): 282.

(53) Potts to HHS, January 14, 1851, and Fred to HHS, January 14 and February 17, 1851, Sibley Papers.

(54) United States Department of Commerce, Bureau of the Census. Seventh (1850) Decennial Census, Mendota, Dakota County, Minnesota Territory.

(55) HHS to Blake, April 29, 1851, and HHS to Sarah A. Sibley, June 15, 1851, Sibley Papers.

(56) HHS to Annie C. Barney Steele, April 21, 1851, Sibley Papers Letterbook.

(57) Sibley Bible, 'births', SHA Collections. HHS to Solomon D. Jacobs, June 15, 1851; and to Trowbridge, August 24, 1851, Sibley Papers.

(58) HHS to Blake, September 6, 1851, Sibley Papers.

(59) HHS to Trowbridge, August 24, 1851; to Borup, September 8 and 17, 1851; to Dousman, September 10, 1851; to Norman W. Kittson, September 15, 1851; and to Martin McLeod, September 15, 1851, Sibley Papers.

(60) HHS to Sarah A. Sibley, September 23, 1851, Sibley Papers. St. Paul *Pioneer &*

Democrat, September 25, 1851. HHS to Ramsay Crooks, September 28, 1851; to John Steele, September 28, 1851; to J.W. McKenny, September 28, 1851; to George Hand, October 1, 1851; to Amos Tuck, October 1, 1851; to Sproat Sibley, October 5, 1851; and to Catherine S. Trowbridge, October 6, 1851, Sibley Papers. SJS, "The Sweet Briar," SHA Collections, 327C.

(61) HHS to Sproat Sibley, October 5, 1851, Sibley Papers.

(62) Potts to HHS, January 18, 1852, Sibley Papers. Family Research Library, "A Genealogical and Historical Study of Major General R.W. Johnson," 2003, online at http://familyresearchlibrary.com/sample_rpt.html (printed copy in author's collection).

(63) SJS to Abbian Potts, January 29, 1852; and to Thomas R. Potts, February 1, 1852, Livingston Papers, Ramsey County Historical Society.

(64) Fred to McKlosky, April 23 and 28, and May 12, 1852, Sibley Papers. Goodman and Goodman, *Paddlewheels*, 135.

(65) Alexander Ramsey diary, June 27, 1852, Ramsey Papers. Goodman and Goodman, *Paddlewheels*, 102.

(66) Rachel E. Johnson to Mary H. Steele, August 26, 1852, Livingston Papers, Ramsey County Historical Society.

(67) HHS to Pierre Chouteau Jr. & Company, September 20, 1852, Sibley Papers. Alexander Ramsey diary, October 24 and 25, 1852, Ramsey Papers.

(68) Fred to Borup, November 17 and 19, 1852, Sibley Papers.

(69) HHS to Borup, December 4, 1852, Sibley Papers.

(70) Fred to HHS, February 27, 1853, Sibley Papers.

(71) Fred to Henry F. McCloskey, April 20, 1853, Sibley Papers.

(72) HHS to Pierre Chouteau Jr. & Company, May 7, 1853 and to Dousman, May 11, 1853, Sibley Papers.

(73) Alexander Ramsey diary, May 19, 1853, Ramsey Papers. HHS to Fred, May 25, 1853, and to McCloskey, June 6, 1853, Sibley Papers.

(74) HHS to McCloskey, June 6 and 14, 1853, Sibley Papers. Katherine C. Grier, *Culture & Comfort: Parlor Making and Middle-Class Identity, 1850-1930* (Washington DC: The Smithsonian Institution Press, 1988): 30-31, 89-116.

(75) HHS to Eastman, June 17, 1853; and, HHS to Borup, June 17, 1853, Sibley Papers. Alexander Ramsey diary, June 19, 1853, Ramsey Papers.

(76) HHS to Charles S. Adams, June 9, 1851; to Joseph LaFramboise Sr., June 8, 1853; and to Pierre Chouteau Jr. & Company, July 15, 1853, Sibley Papers.

(77) HHS to Dousman, and to LeDuc, August 1, 1853, Sibley Papers. Sibley Bible, "births", SHA Collections.

(78) Ellsworth Carlstedt, "Minnesota and the Panic of 1857" (University of Minnesota, Thesis, 1933): 6-41.

(79) HHS to Henry M. Rice, October 2, 1853; and to Trowbridge, October 22, 1853, Sibley Papers. Alexander Ramsey diary, October 26, 1853, Ramsey Papers.

(80) HHS to Robert S. Granger, October 30, 1853, Sibley Papers.

(81) HHS to Ramsey, August 13, 1851; to Blake, January 26, 1854; and to Borup, January 26, 1854, Sibley Papers.

(82) HHS to Rice, February 1, 1854; to Pierre Chouteau Jr. & Company, February 10, 1854; and to Kittson, March 5, 1854, Sibley Papers.

(83) HHS to Sarah A. Sibley, June 15, 1851; and to McCloskey, June 8, 1854, Sibley Papers. Goodman and Goodman, *Paddlewheels*, 1-9.

(84) HHS to McCloskey, June 12, 1854, Sibley Papers.

(85) HHS to Fred, June 20, 1854; and to Trowbridge, July 3, 1854, Sibley Papers.

(86) Mrs. Potts to Potts, July 21, 1854, Livingston Papers, Ramsey County Historical Society. Alexander Ramsey diary, September 16 and 20, 1854, Ramsey Papers.

(87) Alexander Ramsey diary, November 2 and 6, 1854, Ramsey Papers.

(88) HHS to McCloskey, December 25, 1854, Sibley Papers. Alexander Ramsey diary, February 2, 1855, Ramsey Papers.

(89) HHS to Frank, February 3 and 18, 1855, Sibley Papers.

(90) HHS to Chatfield, March 23, 1855; and to Dousman, April 7, 1855, Sibley Papers.

(91) HHS to Borup, April 22 and May 11, 1855, Sibley Papers. Alexander Ramsey diary, June 28, 1855, Ramsey Papers. Sibley Bible, "births", SHA Collection.

(92) Gilman, *Divided Heart*, 130, 141. Doris Kearns Goodwin, *Team of Rivals*, 170-173.

(93) James Shields to Daniel A. Robertson, January 22, 1856, Daniel A. Robertson Papers, MHS. Alexander Ramsey diary, January 17 and January 26, 1856, Ramsey Papers.

(94) Alexander Ramsey diary, February 8, 1856, Ramsey Papers.

(95) SJS to HHS, March 2, 1856, SHA Collection, #250. The year for this letter was fixed by examining a perpetual calendar for Sunday March 2 after the arrival of Gov. Gorman. The letter seems to make sense in the context of Gorman leaving office in 1856, awaiting his replacement, Gov. Samuel Medary.

(96) HHS to Dr. John Steele, February 4, 1856, John Steele Papers, MHS. Carlstedt, "Panic of 1857," 8.

(97) United States Department of Commerce, Census Bureau, Seventh Decennial Census (1850), Strasburg, Pennsylvania. Potts Bible, Sibley House Association Collection.

(98) Alexander Ramsey diary, August 26, 1856, Ramsey Papers.

(99) Stillwater Messenger, March 17 and 24, 1857. Land Grant Jollification, March 17, 1857, Poster Collection, MHS. Alexander Ramsey diary, March 19 and 20, 1857 – Ramsey had recorded the wrong dates – and for James Steele's funeral, March 26, 1857, Ramsey Papers.

(100) Gilman, *Divided Heart*, 148.

(101) Richard W. Johnson to HHS, December 12, 1850, Sibley Papers. Richard W. Johnson, *A Soldier's Reminiscence in Peace and War* (Philadelphia: J.B. Lippencott Co., 1886): 56-92. Rachel E. Johnson to SJS, April 29, 1857, Livingston Papers, Ramsey County Historical Society. Heitman, *Register*, 795, 953, 182, and 894. Susan J. Matt, "You Can't Go Home Again: Homesickness and Nostalgia in U.S. History," *The Journal of American History* 94/2 (September 2007): 476. Bruce A. Kohn, "Wingings of the Bird: Governor Henry Sibley and his daughter Helen," (unpublished manuscript, February 6, 2008): note 204. Kohn cites the Central Park United Methodist Church, November 1863-September 1864.

(102) Alexander Ramsey diary, September 10 and 15, 1857, Ramsey Papers.

(103) Gilman, *Divided Heart*, 153. Alexander Ramsey diary, October 5, 1857, Ramsey Papers. HHS to LeDuc, December 19, 1857, Sibley Papers.

(104) Most of this chapter previously appeared as "First Lady of Preservation: Sarah Sibley and the Mount Vernon Ladies Association" *Minnesota History* 58 (Winter 2003-2004): 407- 416. For discussions of the early roots of Preservation, see W. Barksdale Maynard, "'Best, Lowliest Style!' The Early-Nineteenth-Century Rediscovery of American Colonial Architecture" in *Journal of the Society of Architectural Historians* 59, no. 3 (September 2000): 338-357; Patricia West, *Domesticating History: The Political Origins of America's House Museums* (Washington, DC: Smithsonian Institution Press, 1999): 1-37; and, "The Preservation Movement and the Private Citizen Before World War II" in William J. Murtagh, *Keeping Time: The History and Theory of Preservation in America* (Pittstown, NJ: The Main Street Press, 1988). An example of seeking out Revolutionary sites may be found in Mary M. Crawford, ed., "Mrs. Lydia B. Bacon's Journal, 1811-1812," *Indiana Magazine of History* 40 (1944): 370.

(105) Earle S. Goodrich in St. Paul *Daily Pioneer*, June 6, 1854. For a discussion of the Preservation movement in Minnesota, see Russell W. Fridley's introduction in June Drenning Holmquist and Jean A. Brookins, *Minnesota's Major Historic Sites: A Guide* (St. Paul, MN: MHS Press, 1972; Second Edition). See also Ann Marcaccini and George M. Woytanowitz, "House Work: the DAR at the Sibley House" *Minnesota History* 55 (Spring 1997): 186-201.

(106) Christie Johnson to William Markoe, October 1, 1858, William Markoe and Family Papers, courtesy Sara Markoe Hanson.

(107) Johnson to Markoe, October 1, 1858, Markoe Papers. Christie Johnson to Mary Morris Hamilton, October 20, 1858. Mount Vernon Ladies Association, Mount Vernon, Virginia. Early Association Records. (MVLA) Hamilton is the granddaughter of Alexander Hamilton and the niece of Gouverneur Morris. Edward W. Callahan, *List of Officers of the Navy or the United States and the*

Marine Corps from 1775 to 1900 (Washington: Government Printing Office, 1901; repr. Haskell House Publishers, 1969): 170.

(108) For a detailed discussion of changes to women's rights in the mid-nineteenth century, see Glenna Matthews, *The Rise of Public Woman: Woman's Power and Woman's Place in the United States, 1630-1970* (New York: Oxford University Press, 1992): 93-146.

(109) SJS to Ann Pamela Cunningham, November 28, 1858, MVLA.

(110) St. Paul *Pioneer & Democrat*, June 22, 1859.

(111) St. Paul *Pioneer*, September 4, 1858. Kohn, "Wingings of the Bird," chapter 1 contains a through description of the day.

(112) SJS to Ann Pamela Cunningham, April 1, 1859, MVLA. SJS to Mary Bronson LeDuc, March 13, 1859, LeDuc Papers. William Gates LeDuc to HHS, May 12, 1859, Sibley Papers.

(113) Charles H. Berry to Francis Eliza Hubbell Berry, December 12, 1859. Charles H. Berry Papers, MHS. Ann Loomis North to Anne Lewis, March 30, 1859, John W. North Papers, Huntington Library (California), on microfilm copy at MHS. John W. North to HHS, December 2, 1858, Sibley Papers.

(114) *Saint Paul Pioneer & Democrat*, February 22, 1859.

(115) The day's planning and activities are chronicled in the following: St. Paul *Pioneer & Democrat*, February 18, February 19, February 22, and February 24, 1859; St. Paul *Daily Times*, February 24, 1859; and St. Paul *Weekly Minnesotian*, February 26, 1859. SJS to Edward Everett, May 11, 1859, Everett-Norcross Collection, Massachusetts Historical Society. Edward Everett to SJS, May 19, 1859, Sibley Papers.

(116) Stillwater *Messenger*, May 3 and 10, 1859. Stillwater *Democrat*, April 30, 1859. Unfortunately, the May 7 issue of the *Democrat* is not in the MHS collections.

(117) Stillwater *Messenger*, March 8, 1859. St. Anthony *Falls Evening News*, March 19, 1859. Hastings *Independent*, February 24, 1859 and April 12, 1859. St. Peter *Minnesota Statesman*, March 16, 1859. Winona *Republican*, March 2, 1859. Faribault *Central Republican*, March 9, 1859.

(118) St. Paul *Pioneer & Democrat*, June 7, 1859. George L. Lumsden to SJS in St. Paul *Pioneer & Democrat*, February 22, 1859. *Mount Vernon Record* (October 1859): 21. George Lumsden's wife might be remembered for allegedly harboring convicted murderer Anne Bilansky during her brief escape from prison later that summer. Bilansky was the only woman ever executed in Minnesota; both Gov. Sibley and Gov. Ramsey refused to pardon her.

(119) *Mount Vernon Record* (October 1859): 21. United States. Bureau of the Census. Eighth Decennial Census, Mendota Township, Dakota County, Minnesota, June 19, 1860, microfilm copy, MHS.

(120) HHS to John H. Stevens, May 31 and August 4, 1859, Stevens Papers, MHS. St. Paul *Pioneer & Democrat*, June 3, 1859.

(121) SJS to Mary Bronson LeDuc, March 13, 1859, LeDuc Papers, MHS. SJS to Ann Pamela Cunningham, July 29, 1859, MVLA.

(122) Benedict Schmid Diary, Harriet Nubson Papers, Carver County Historical Society. SJS to Ann Pamela Cunningham, July 29, 1859, MVLA. R. Junius and Abby Mendenhall Papers, Diary, 1858-1859, MHS.

(123) Sylvester Sawyer to William R. Brown, 1860, Brown Papers, MHS. Rebecca Marshall Cathcart interview, September 15, 1904, (vol. 82) in William Watts Folwell Papers.

(124) Charles Berry to Frances Eliza Hubbell Berry, December 12, 1859, Berry Papers, MHS.

(125) SJS to Ann Pamela Cunningham, January 23, 1860, MVLA. Mount Vernon Ladies Association, Annual Report. 1889: 6-7.

(126) Rice to Annie Steele, August 29, 1858; and Stevens to Steele, January 13, 1860, Franklin Steele Papers, MHS. Gilman, *Divided Heart*, 162-163.

(127) HHS to Ann Pamela Cunningham, April 19, 1860, MVLA.

(128) James M. McPherson, *Battle Cry of Freedom: The Civil War Era* (New York: Oxford University Press, 1988): 213-216. Rhoda R. Gilman, *Henry Hastings Sibley; Divided Heart* (St. Paul: Minnesota Historical Society Press, 2004): 162-165.

(129) HHS to William G. LeDuc, July 23, 1860, LeDuc Papers.

(130) Sibley Bible, "births", SHA Collections.

(131) HHS to Ann Pamela Cunningham, October 20, 1860, MVLA.

(132) HHS to LeDuc, January 3, 1861, Sibley Papers, MHS.

(133) Alexander Ramsey diary, March 1, 1861, Ramsey Papers. HHS to Z. Pitcher, August 21, 1851, Sibley Papers.

(134) Goodrich to HHS, March 16, 1861, Sibley Papers. HHS to LeDuc, March 23, 1861, LeDuc Papers.

(135) For information on the change in American life in the Civil War era, see James M. McPherson, *Battle Cry of Freedom*. Richard W. Johnson, "War Memories, by R. W. Johnson, Brevet Major-General, U.S. Army," in *Glimpses of the Nation's Struggle*, a series of papers read before the Minnesota Commandery of the Military Order of the Loyal Legion of the United States (St. Paul: St. Paul Book and Stationery Company, 1887): 9.

(136) Johnson, "War Memories," 7-9.

(137) Family Research Library, "A Genealogical and Historical Study of Major General R.W. Johnson."

(138) HHS to Charles H. Berry, July 3, 1861, Berry Papers.

(139) SJS to Rachel Johnson, November 17, 1861, Sibley Papers. Undated news item from Sibley House. Annie Steele diary, January 1, 1869. Augusta Ann

Sibley to Carrie Gullagher, February 17, 1856, Sibley House Association Collections, #307.

(140) Henry Moss to Edward D. Neill, December 13, 1861, Neill Papers, MHS. Alexander Ramsey diary, January 23, 1862.

(141) Alexander Ramsey diary, June 12, 1862, Ramsey Papers.

(142) Alexander Ramsey diary, August 19, 1862, Ramsey Papers.

(143) Frank Moore, ed. *Women of the War: Their Heroism and Self-Sacrifice.* Hartford: S. S. Scranton & Co., 1866. There are many other more recent works on women in the Civil War, but Moore's published in the wake of the war provides a fairly comprehensive sense of women's experiences in their own words.

(144) St. Paul *Pioneer & Democrat* and St. Paul *Daily Press* Tuesday November 18, 1862. HHS to John H. Thurston, December 23, 1878, John Thurston Papers, MHS. HHS to Franklin Steele, August 21, 1862, Franklin Steele Papers, MHS. Stephen E. Osman, *Fort Snelling during the Civil War* (draft in author's possession, forthcoming monograph): 156-157 (accounts of soldier misbehavior in Mendota).

(145) St. Paul *Daily Dispatch*, May 21, 1869.

(146) St. Paul *Pioneer*, December 11, 1862. St. Paul City Directory, 1863. Eileen R. McCormack, "Lost Neighborhood: Mary Hill's Lowertown, 1867-1891" *Ramsey County History* 41/1 (Spring 2006): 4. Alexander Ramsey diary, December 12, 1862, January 1, 16, and 22, February 8, and March 3, 1863, Ramsey Papers.

(147) Alexander Ramsey diary, May 28, 1863, Ramsey Papers. Sibley Family Bible, Sibley House Association Collection, MHS. St. Paul City Directory, 1864. St. Paul City Ward Map, 1865. Sanborn Fire Insurance Map, 1885.

(148) McCormack, "Lost Neighborhood: Mary Hill's Lowertown, 1867-1891," *Ramsey County History* 41/1 (Spring 2006): 6-7.

(149) HHS diary, June 13, 1863, Sibley Papers.

(150) St. Paul *Pioneer*, July 20, 1863. Sibley Bible, "births", SHA Collections.

(151) Ramsey County Register of Deeds, Book EE, p. 178, at MHS.

(152) For more on Lowertown see: Marshall R. Hatfield, "Once Upon a Time – 'Tasteful and Elegant': Lafayette Park and the vanished homes of St. Paul's Elite," *Ramsey County History* 29/2 (Summer 1994): 4-21. Delores Hayden, *Building Suburbia: Green Fields and Urban Growth, 1820-2000* (New York: Pantheon Books, 2003): 21-70. McCormack, "Lost Neighborhood," 4.

(153) Martha D. Bass reminiscence, typescript c. 1900, p. 23, in Jacob W. Bass Papers, MHS. See Carlstedt, "Minnesota and the Panic of 1857," 59.

(154) Alexander Ramsey diary, August 16, 1864, Ramsey Papers. Anna Ramsey to Mary LeDuc, September 2, 1864, LeDuc Papers.

(155) HHS to William Markoe, December 18, 1866, MVLA.

(156) Richard Johnson to HHS, Friday August 31, 1866, Sibley Papers. Interview with Sandy Elmstrom, February 8, 2006. Mrs. Elmstrom is the great-great-granddaughter of Sarah Sibley, and she believed that there were a number of miscarriages from stories told in the family. R. Sauer, "Attitudes to Abortion in America, 1800-1973," *Population Studies* 28/1 (March 1974): 54. Pearson Education, Inc. "Crude Birth and Death Rates for Selected Countries," 2006. 2006 data for the United States compiled from the U.S. Census Bureau. Steven A. Camarota, "Birth Rates Among Immigrants in America: Comparing Fertility in the U. S. and Home Countries," *Center for Immigration Studies*, (October 2005): 1.

(157) All data from US Census for years 1849, 1850, 1857, 1860, and MN Census 1865. For the 1857 and 1860 censuses it is difficult to distinguish between residents of Mendota and residents of Mendota Township, thus all were used. For the 1865 Minnesota Census, 15 households enumerated either side of the Sibley family were used.

(158) All data from US Census for years 1849, 1850, 1857, 1860, and MN Census 1865. The families use were Jacob and Martha Bass, George and Susannah Becker, Charles and Elizabeth Borup, William and Catherine Forbes, William and Ellen Hollinshead, William and Maria Markoe, Charles Oakes, Thomas and Abby Potts, John S. Prince, Alexander and Anna Ramsey, Edmund and Anne Rice, Henry and Mathilda Rice, Daniel and Julia Robertson, Howard and H.M. Stansbury, Frank and Annie Steele, John and Catherine Steele, and John H. Stevens.

(159) R. Sauer, "Attitudes to Abortion in America, 1800-1973," 54-55. John Todd, *Serpents in the Dove's Nest* (Boston: Lee and Shepard, 1867): 4, (quote) 6.

(160) St. Paul *Pioneer*, November 15, 1867. St. Paul *Dispatch*, November 16, 1907, "40 Years Ago." HHS to Hercules Dousman, December 4 and December 17, 1867, Sibley Papers.

(161) Annie Steele diary, September 7 to 24, 1868, Annie Steele Papers.

(162) St. Paul *Pioneer*, December 1864. Stephen E. Osman, "Ode to the Laurel Pipe," unpublished paper, 2006. Dean R. Thilgen, "Early Minnesota Base Ball" unpublished paper, 2004.

(163) Annie Steele diary September 25 to 26, 1868, Annie Steele Papers.

(164) Anna Barney Steele diary, September 29, October 2 and 11, 1868, Anna Barney Steele Papers. HHS to Henry Whipple, September 29, 1868, Sibley Papers.

(165) SJS to Mary Bronson LeDuc, April 30, 1869, LeDuc Papers.

(166) St. Paul *Daily Dispatch*, May 21, 1869. St. Paul *Pioneer*, May 22, 1869.

(167) St. Paul *Daily Dispatch*, May 22, 1869. St. Paul *Pioneer*, May 24, 1869.

(168) Alexander Ramsey diary May 25, 1869, Ramsey Papers.

(169) John Fletcher Williams, "Memoir of Henry Hastings Sibley," *Minnesota*

Historical Society Collections 6 (St. Paul: The Pioneer Press Company, 1894): 303.

(170) MVLA Annual Report, 1889. Marcaccini and Woytanowitz, "House Work," 186-201.

(171) Wilmer W. MacElree, *Around the Boundaries of Chester County* (West Chester, PA: n.p., 1934): 77. J. Smith Furthey and Gilbert Cope, *History of Chester County, Pennsylvania, with Genealogies and Biographical Sketches* (Philadelphia: Louis A. Everts, 1881): 730. Samuel T. Wiley, *Biographical and Portrait Cyclopedia of Chester County*, revised and edited by Winfield Scott Garner (Philadelphia: Gresham Publishing Company, 1893): 160.

(172) McCormack, "Lost Neighborhood," 4-9. David Riehle, "Lowertown: Another Perspective," *Ramsey County History* 41/1 (Spring 2006): 10-11. Marshall R. Hatfield, "Once Upon a Time – 'Tasteful, Elegant': Lafayette Park and the Vanished Homes of St. Paul's Elite," *Ramsey County History* 29/2 (Summer 1994): 4-21. Woytanowitz, *Chronicle*, 1892.

(173) Julia M. Johnson, "Mrs. Sarah Jane Sibley," 25-26.

(174) St. Paul *Daily Dispatch*, May 21, 1869. Christopher Columbus Andrews, ed. *History of St. Paul, Minnesota, with illustrations and biographical sketches of some of its prominent men and pioneers* part 2 (Syracuse, NY: D. Mason & Company, 1890): 23. Williams, "Memoir of Henry Hastings Sibley," 270. Charles E. Flandrau, *Encyclopedia of Biography of Minnesota* (Chicago: The Century Publishing and Engraving Company, 1900): 466.

(175) Julia M. Johnson, "Mrs. Sarah Jane Sibley," 25-26. Mary Dillon Foster, ed. *Who's Who Among Minnesota Women: a history of women's work in Minnesota from pioneer days to date, told in biographies, memorial and records of organizations.* (Mary Dillon Foster, 1924): 297.

Apendix A: Tables for Chapter 8

Table 8.1

Neighbor-Households near Sarah Jane Sibley, 1849-1865 (157)

	Total Households	Average Household Size	Sibley Household Size	Average Males/Household	Average Females/Household
1849	35	3.57	11	2.03	1.54
1850	29	4.90	11	2.97	1.93
1857	48	5.83	11	3.42	2.42
1860	87	5.16	12	2.71	2.45
1865	30	4.37	10	2.14	2.24

Table 8.2

Social Peer-Households of Sarah Jane Sibley, 1849-1865 (158)

	Total Households	Average Household Size	Sibley Household Size	Average Males/Household	Average Females/Household
1849	4	7.34	11	3.34	4.00
1850	11	6.40	11	3.40	3.00
1857	11	8.10	11	3.00	5.10
1860	12	9.00	12	3.64	4.82
1865	10	8.66	10	3.34	5.34

Six Miles from St. Paul

Appendix B: Poems by Sarah Jane Sibley

Pleasure and Desire

In yonder bower lies Pleasure sleeping
And near him mourns a blooming maid.
He will not wake and she sits weeping
When lo! A stranger proffers aid.

His hurried step, his glances of fire
The god of wishes wild declare;
"Wake, Pleasure, wake!" exclaims Desire,
And Pleasure wakes to bless the fair.

But soon the maid in luckless hour
Desire asleep is doomed to view;
"Try, Pleasure, try!" she cries, "your power,
[line missing in the original]

Fond girl, thy prayer exceeds all measure,
Distinct his province each must keep,
Desire shall never wait on Pleasure,
And Pleasure hold Desire to sleep.

Hymn to the Virgin

Ave Maria! Maiden mild

Listen to a maiden's prayer;

Six Miles from St. Paul

Thou canst hear though from the wild

Thou canst save amid despair

Safe may we sleep beneath thy care,

Though banished, outcast, and reviled –

Mother, hear a supplicant child

Ave Maria

Ave Maria! Undefiled

The flinty couch we must not share

Shall seem with down of eider piled

If thy protection hover there,

The murky cavern's heavy air

Shall breathe of balm if thou hast smiled;

Thou Maiden! Hear a maiden's prayer,

Mother, list a supplicant child:

Ave Maria

Ave Maria! Stainless styled!

Foul demons of the earth and air

From this their worsted haunt exiled

Shall flee before thy presence fair.

We bow us to our lot of care,

Beneath thy guidance reconciled;

Hear for a maid a maiden's prayer,

And for a father hear a child

Ave Maria

Six Miles from St. Paul

The Sweet Briar

Our sweet autumnal western scented wind

Robs odours none so sweet a flower

In all the blooming waste it left behind

As that the sweet briar yields it; and the shower

Wets not a rose that binds in beauty's bower

One half so lonely; yet it grows along

The poor girl's pathway by the man's door,

Such are the simple folks it dwells among;

And humble as the bred, so humble be the song.

I love it for it takes its untouched stand

Not in the vase that sculptors decorate;

Its sweetness all is of my native land;

And in its fragrant leaf has not its mate

Among the perfumes which the rich and great

Buy from the odours of the spring East

You love your flowers and plant and will you hate

His little four leaf rose that I love best,

That freshest will awake, and sweetest go to rest?

As in the storm that pours destruction sound

Is here and there a ship in safety found;

   Lo, in the storms of life, some days appear

More blest and bright for the preceding fear:

These times of pleasure that in life arise,

Like spots in deserts, that delight, surprise,

And to our wearied senses give the more,

For all the waste behind us and before.

Six Miles from St. Paul

Appendix C: Known Sibley Household Staff

Much more study should be undertaken on domestic servants in the Sibley's employ.

Brooks, male – African-American waiter (Campbell to HHS, 1849)

Chevellier, Francis – 38 (1850 US Census)

Church, Maria – 25, native of Ireland (1857 MN Statehood Census)

Dolan, Susan (1865 MN State Census)

Dunn, Walter – 18, native of Ireland (1857, 1860 Census)

Lord, Joseph – 82 (1850 US Census)

Louvcat, Roselle – 17, native of France (1850 US Census)

Murphy, John (1865 MN State Census)

Murphy, Maggie (1865 MN State Census, burned to death in 1867)

Nebila, Mary – 24, native of Ireland (1860 US Census)

O'Brien, Catherine – 40, native of Ireland (1850 US Census)

Pampe, Eloi – 25, native of Canada (1857, 1860 Census)

Robertson, Ellen – 28, native of Scotland (1857, 1860 Census)

Robinson, Joe – African-American cook, pre-1840s (Gilman, 64)

Russell, Roswell P. (*Old Rail Fence Corners*, 306)

Shields, John – farmhand (SJS to HHS, 1856)

Thomas, Mary A. (1865 MN State Census)

Index

Names of people